THE INVISIBLE
INK SERIES

TEACHING FOR CHARACTER

SUPER-CHARGED LEARNING THROUGH THE 'INVISIBLE CURRICULUM'

ANDREW HAMMOND

First Published 2015

by John Catt Educational Ltd,
12 Deben Mill Business Centre,
Old Maltings Approach,
Melton, Woodbridge IP12 1BL

Tel: +44 (0) 1394 389850
Fax: +44 (0) 1394 386893
Email: enquiries@johncatt.com
Website: www.johncatt.com

ISBN: 978 1 909717 343

Set and designed by Theoria Design.

Contents

Foreword
by Max Coates

When you Google quotations from Einstein there are so many that you wonder how he found time to develop his theory of relativity. My favourite (obligatory?) quotation of his is "Everybody is a genius. But if you judge a fish by its ability to climb a tree, it will live its whole life believing that it is stupid." This book just resonates with Einstein's scathing observation on what we do to people, and children in particular. Of course if we take relativity seriously it could be that it is the other way round!

One of the most bizarre phenomena is that we repeatedly castigate our education system. It is argued that it is not as good as Finland or that we need to look to Singapore to develop effective Mathematics teaching. Yet, there is a counter current of educationalists coming to the UK to learn about innovation and how to develop creativity. As a nation we behave as if we are an egocentric toddler by grasping at what others in the playgroup have without appreciating the worth of what we are actually holding.

The value of this book is that Andrew has joined the ranks of a minority of educational authors who are committed to keeping the story of education alive. As you read the book you will sense his passion to release and cultivate the wellspring of education that lies with character. He speaks of a substrata of intelligence which he calls 'invisible ink'. These facets are itemised and clear strategies for their propagation are considered. The book is deeply subversive as he seeks to spill this ink and not merely blot it up or screw the lid on the bottle like so much current education practice attempts to do. There is an unashamed polemic to recognise the need to place the child at the heart of education.

The book is peppered with stories and these score points throughout. As an academic educationalist they cause me to re-engage with the excitement of teaching and its effective design and construction. No story is gratuitous though I would like to speak to Henry (see Chapter 1) and suggest that he cuts a deal for a share of his father's royalties.

Reading 'Teaching for Character' is a bit like visiting Madame Tussauds, though probably much cheaper. You are transported to a 'hall of fame' the influential and in many cases almost forgotten are resurrected; Bruner, Montessori, Dewey, Locke, Rousseau, Piaget and Gelb. These are not past masters who have been superseded but prophets whose message needs to be reawakened. Andrew has certainly got the defibrillator out!

There are now a plethora of routes into teaching including Teach First, Teach Direct and just walk through the door. This book ought to be mandatory reading for all who want to nurture the thinking and learning of children and young people (and adults if it comes to that, just think what it would do to a professional development day). It is the antidote to the great march backwards to a sort of Victorian approach to teaching with a touch of IT.

Andrew, thank you for writing this book – it is beyond being timely.

Max Coates

Senior Lecturer in Education at University College London / Institute of Education.

1 Invisible Ink

I am not a scientist. I bunked off too many science lessons at school, preferring to hide in my Dad's shed on his neighbouring allotment, with a starter pack of Silk Cut and a box of matches padded out with tissue to prevent an incriminating rattle. The shed was warm and cosy and I could spy on my compliant classmates up in the science block from a small crack in the shed wall. Tobacco smoke, combined with the earthy smells of compost and potatoes, all neatly chitting on the shelf, must have made for a furtive whiff when I got back.

I wish I'd known then what I know now. Not only about the dangers of smoking, but about the perils of ignoring what was going on in those science lessons. Science and I parted company thirty years ago. Luckily we've recently become reacquainted. Turns out it's more exciting than my old man's allotment shed.

In order to make up for lost ground, and in penance for the truancies and the cigarettes of a misspent youth, I recently set myself the task of trying to understand quantum mechanics. An ambitious task, perhaps.

I can think of three reasons to explain why QM is so very difficult to comprehend. Firstly, it is describing something that is entirely hidden from view and, in many respects, counter-intuitive to our classical view of the world around us. Secondly, it is explained in language that belongs to the era of classical science – it's like using English to describe the English language to an alien, or lighting a stadium with a pocket torch. And thirdly, I must have been in my Dad's shed for that particular lesson.

Before the twentieth century, a classical view of science held that the description of the nature of an object and the measurement of that object were the *same thing.*

Reality was as you measured it to be. If you could identify what an object is made from then you could accurately describe its state, its existence in the universe. We now find that such a theory fails spectacularly at the subatomic level. When cleverer men than I discovered that particles of mass can behave like a particle *and* a wave (with no mass) at the same time, then everything changed forever and the modern, technology-rich world as we know it today, but unimaginable a century ago, was born. The concept of accurate measurement was replaced with the invisible concepts of potential and probability. As Jim Baggott (2011) says in his extraordinary *The Quantum Story*, 'we began with the certainties of knowledge and ended with the knowledge of absolute uncertainty'.

I cannot explain the quantum world in any more detail other than to say there is an invisible quality to the existence of things: a relationship between mass and energy, and a reaction to the environment in which things exists, that means, in theory, anything and everything can happen. We cannot perceive reality as it really is, only as it seems in response to the questions we ask of it and the measurements we take.

And so it is with education. There are many elements of teaching and learning that remain hidden from view, and the language we use to try to describe these invisible elements belongs to an era in which only the visible counted. The measurements we take must not be misinterpreted as the only truth, or else the law of self-fulfilling prophecies applies. (Take the humble word *progress*, for example: it suggests advancement towards an established, visible goal, and yet none of us know where our pupils' trajectories are headed. None of us know their potential. None of us can see their energy. Perhaps that's why I've always preferred the word *development* instead: it suggests growth from the root, rather than advancement to a pre-ordained height).

With apologies to any scientists reading this, let us assume the examinable aspect of a child's intelligence is his 'nucleus'. His energy and potential we shall call the 'electron'. We teach, weigh and measure the nucleus of the child with great regularity and assume this is an accurate description of the child and his ability. It's not. It's not at all. The weighing of the nucleus gives little regard for the potential of the charmingly unpredictable electron encircling it, and yet it is this little fellow that will have greatest impact on the child's output: yesterday, now, tomorrow and in the future. No-one can accurately predict what that child is capable of saying, writing, doing or being, not today, not tomorrow, not ever.

To suggest that a child's actual ability and potential can be encapsulated in his predicted grades for GCSE, or his Common Entrance results, or his row of A*s at A level is as absurd as suggesting that the state of an object can be defined and described with certainty through classical measurement. Or that your torch can reveal every seat in the stadium.

Or it's as absurd as saying that a Formula One racing car's performance is defined by its position on the leaderboard. Rather, this is the *result* of its performance on a given day and in response to a particular environment. Its actual performance has to do with how it is running – its tyres, its engine, its aerodynamics, the driver's skill, the driver's concentration levels, the driver's motivation and mood, and not to mention the environment in which the car finds itself: the movements of the other cars, the intentions of their drivers, the weather, the surface, the unexpected actions of the crowd, and so on. There are so many variables, so many observables. In theory, the car could win any race or lose any race; it could spin, leave the ground or, God forbid, burst into flames the moment it leaves the starting grid. It has incalculable potential.

To say the result that a car achieves in a race *is* its performance is to miss all the opportunities the race team engineers have to improve the car next time. If they focused only on the leaderboard position – the visible results of the car's performance – they'd pack up their spanners and go home. Job done. The challenge – and the excitement, one assumes – comes from analysing what worked, what failed, and what can be finely tuned for an improved performance next time.

And so it is with education, again. A growth mindset, rather than a fixed one, lies at the heart of good teaching and learning, and yet so much of schooling seems hell-bent on delivering fixed measurements, and then calling them 'performance'. It's hard to maintain a growth mindset when you're knee deep in summative assessment scores, printed indelibly on your academic report. The language we use to report on children's 'progress' through school is concerned with the measurable: assessment, attainment, lower and higher ability, and so on. I used to think I was pleasingly progressive when, in various leadership roles, I encouraged colleagues to use the word 'journey' more often. It's the journey that matters, and so on. It is only now that I realise 'journey' assumes an intended destination too. The word adventure would have been better. Perhaps schools should be renamed 'adventure centres'; the assonance alone would win over critics.

As Maria Montessori put it,

> If education is always to be conceived along the same antiquated lines of a mere transmission of knowledge, there is little to be hoped from it in the bettering of man's future. For what is the use of transmitting knowledge if the individual's total development lags behind? (Montessori, 1949: 4)

What lies behind an A grade in French, after all? Or a B in History? How was it achieved? This is only the visible element – the physical examination paper with etchings on it – the downloading from a term spent genning-up. But the grade itself can all too easily become the accepted description of the child's ability – the classical measurement. If you get on the leaderboard you're a success and if you don't you're not. The proof is there to see – you're a B or a D or 120 VR or a 96 NVR. The little, enigmatic electron is nowhere to be seen.

I've always enjoyed a delightful quote from Alfred Binet, father of the IQ test: 'Intelligence, like love or beauty, is immeasurable.' In quantum terms, I guess it's uncertain, unpredictable and dynamic; there is a great deal that is hidden from view. There is much more behind that A grade than the child's computational capacity or his mastery of the 3Rs (to receive, remember and regurgitate) on a given day. The results of an exam cannot, unfortunately, be attributed solely to the extent to which the pupil listened and worked hard in class or crammed the night before. There is an infinite number of variables at play. An infinite number of observables. There is his character, his motivation, his levels of curiosity and interest in the subject, his rapport with the teacher, his mood on the day... and so on. It is these invisible elements that combine to create immeasurable potential in every child.

Often, when I have attended parents' evenings for any of my four children and have asked how each of them has performed, the teacher has referred to my child's recent examination results (parents' evenings so often follow exams, don't they?) and told me that my child has performed 'very well' in English or Geography, or even Science in the case of my eldest son, Henry (I resisted renting an allotment next to his school for fear of distraction). The evidence for this conclusion is the

A grade marked against my son's name on the list of examination results in the teacher's hand.

Had I been granted more than the obligatory five minutes in the speed-dating whirl of a parents' evening, I would have said, 'I'm sorry, when I asked how has Henry performed, I meant how has he performed in class this term? I didn't mean what grade has his learning performance yielded in the latest round of examinations. That would be a different question, wouldn't it?'

It would be hypocritical of me to suggest that I have not reached for the same sheet of assessment results when a parent has enquired about their child's performance during my seventeen years of teaching. Of course I have – because it has often been the only hard evidence I have had to hand. Or at least the only evidence that is visible and quick and can be communicated in a five-minute speed date. A more prosaic exposition of a child's learning habits would take much longer and is going to be – and this is the real nub of the problem – harder to see, harder to measure and harder to comment on using the traditional language of school, our inherited lexicon of *progress*, *assessment* and *attainment*, which flounders when trying to describe character, or motivation or curiosity or potential, and emanates from the dictionary of fixed mindsets.

In briefing parents on their daughter's academic progress, can you imagine the reaction if I had said, 'Well, Mr and Mrs Jenkins, of course we all know that intelligence, like love or beauty, is immeasurable, so I can't really tell you. But isn't that liberating?'

A teacher must demonstrate that his or her pupils are making progress towards the required standards. A school must deliver the grades its pupils need in order to access the next tier of their education, which, coincidentally, will be predicated on earning grades to access the next level, which in turn is focused on gaining the grades needed to access the next level again. And the next. Until, in a glorious graduation, the student enters the adult world only to find that grades were only half the story.

When renowned business leaders stand up and tell us that our education system is failing to deliver graduates who possess the aptitudes and attitudes needed in the workplace I'm tempted to retort, 'Of course. Our formal education system was never designed to deliver those things; what did you expect?' As Ken Robinson says in his *Out of our Minds,* 'It's like buying a bus and complaining that it sank.'

I believe that our formal education system, as we know it, is predicated on certain historical assumptions about the purpose of education, which were made when mass education first came into being:

1. The most effective way to bring about success for a society and its economy is to develop the intelligence of its younger generation.

2. The most accurate measure of intelligence, and therefore a predictor of future success, both for the individual and for the economy, is academic qualification.

3. The best way to incentivise students to study for academic qualifications is through a system of external rewards and sanctions, and the best way to chart their progress is by examination.

I believe these assumptions are flawed for a variety of reasons. Firstly, when intelligence and academicism are conflated, other forms of intelligence – equally important for future success and equally valuable to employers in a post-industrial labor market – are filtered out.

Secondly, a school curriculum which leads to academic qualifications sifts subjects and abilities into 'useful' and 'non-useful' categories, those that are examined and those that are not, thus creating a hierarchical approach to learning and pupil development.

Thirdly, the delivery of a rigid, academic syllabus (with knowledge, skills and concepts to be taught, learned and examined) creates a stultifying classroom experience and a culture non-conducive to natural curiosity, creativity and the character traits and attitudes most likely to bring about success and well-being.

And finally, one of the most destructive forces to inhibit a child's natural curiosity and creative potential is the pressure exerted by external rewards and sanctions. Extrinsic motivation seldom produces the same quality or quantity of work as its cousin, intrinsic motivation, which is derived from deep engagement in, and ownership of, a learning activity, when the creator sees meaning and purpose in what they are doing (beyond the rewards/sanctions if they succeed/fail).

This series of books will attempt to do more than complain about the traditional school system we have inherited. It will provide practical advice and suggestions for delivering on those all-important academic qualifications *at the same time as* nurturing curiosity, creativity, motivation and those character traits and attitudes that are so important to prosperity and well-being, far beyond the school gates.

The Department for Education's current *Teachers' Standards* clearly recognise the importance of such development in addition to academic progress. Such standards by no means focus only teaching academic knowledge and skills; they state that a teacher must establish stimulating environments, encourage positive attitudes, promote a love of learning and foster intellectual curiosity. And the onus to demonstrate proof that these aims are being met lies with the teacher – and, in some schools, is scrutinised through their performance management. So it must happen and it must be evidenced.

But I shall resist the temptation to propose a structured, measurable programme for assessing and reporting on those invisible elements. Heaven forbid my daughter returning home saying that her Curiosity grade has slipped from an A to a B minus.

With science enjoying such dominance over the arts, the consequence of which has led to an obsession with measurable evidence, I worry that in debating how we develop character, or curate curiosity or encourage creativity, we are drawn to the inevitable question, 'How do we assess it?'

This dominance of science over the arts is reflected in most curricula around the world. It is difficult to deny that we too have inherited a hierarchy in which academic subjects enjoy a higher status, and more curriculum time, than creative subjects. When I was a Director of Studies I dolloped out that most precious commodity – time – to each subject across the timetable in the usual manner: five scoops for English, five for Maths, five for Science, three scoops for MFL, two scoops for History, and so on, until you reached Drama and PSHE which made do with half a scoop between them (or the morsels of time still stuck to the scoop). As a consequence, the ability to receive, remember and regurgitate academic knowledge on demand is deemed to be of greater importance than the ability to work as part of a team, or use one's initiative, or express oneself creatively, or envision solutions to problems, or cope with uncertainty, or feel empathy for others or show kindness and tolerance. Perhaps this is why one hundred years ago this year, John Dewey wrote:

> From the standpoint of the child, the great waste in the school comes from his inability to utilise the experiences he gets outside school in any complete and free way within the school itself; while, on the other hand, he is unable to apply in daily life what he is learning in school. (Dewey, 1915: 47).

The constant need for evidence of progress, measured against established targets and predictions, means that science and logic and reason and meaning will always enjoy more attention than the Arts which are, by definition, harder to codify and assess. It is a wonder, then, that the word 'play' has managed to survive in our lexicon at all. We have the very sound thinking of the early years education to thank for this, perhaps – more on which in later chapters.

And still, a century on from Dewey, the disconnect persists; but any school that chooses not to perpetuate the same hierarchy of academic intelligence over other forms of intelligence (which may have more application outside school) will fail. I sometimes wonder whether the real purpose of school is to prepare students for… the world of school. By the time my children finish their education they will have developed all the learning skills and amassed all the academic knowledge they need to be able to succeed in school. Perhaps they should become teachers or university professors then?

But, oh, how the world is full of pundits and spectators all gazing at education and telling those of us within it what we are doing wrong! But not enough people are giving us solutions to the problems and inadequacies which they politely, and often engagingly, highlight for us. We *know* a learning revolution is required; we *know* that our inherited education system is predicated on industrial-era thinking that lacks relevance today; and we *know* that the system we're using isn't delivering the skills and attitudes needed for tomorrow's world of work. We don't need anyone else to tell us this any more. When you point out the lack of solutions emitting from certain critics of our current education system, they will retort that it is not their role to provide them; they are merely catalysts for change, the interlocutors.

That's a cop out. We need solutions. And what we really need is practical ideas to help us deliver the aptitudes and attitudes needed for the modern world of work within the system that we currently have – because we're not going to change it overnight. And we need ideas for how to evidence that it is happening.

This series will not be another teacher-bashing tome, aimed at pointing out the flaws in the current system – such a crusade is old hat now. We could round up those responsible for creating our traditional education system of teaching to examinations and throw squashed tomatoes at them on the village green, but they are long dead and buried – perhaps that is just the point.

And we shall never create a learning revolution by knocking the very teachers who are trying to do the best they can with what they have inherited – the heroes who work tirelessly to equip children with twenty-first century skills using nineteenth century tools and in an environment that often resembles a nineteenth century clerk's office.

I know of not a single teacher who believes the current educational system is without flaws and who is motivated by the tantalising prospect of teaching children 'out of creativity' rather than into it, or robbing them of the awe and wonder with which they were factory-fitted at birth. No teacher I have ever met has been motivated by robbing children of their innate creativity or curiosity; it is just the system we have inherited. But at the very least, we can work within the system to ensure that our teaching is more 'in sync' with the natural rhythms of childhood. As Jerome Bruner tells us,

> 'The task of teaching a subject to a child at any particular age is one of representing the structure of that subject in terms of the child's way of viewing things.' (1977: 33).

Such an aim is reflected in the current version of the DfE's *Teachers' Standards*, which state that a teacher must:

> Demonstrate an awareness of the physical, social and intellectual development of children, and know how to adapt teaching to support pupils' education at different stages of development. (DfE, 2011: 11)

Viewing lesson objectives through the eyes of a child may be a good place to start. Greater changes take time and can only come from a place of trust rather than distrust – optimism rather than pessimism. A growth mindset rather than a fixed one.

And it can only be achieved by sharing wisdom rather than scare stories; and by wisdom, I mean '**W**hat **I** **S**hall **D**o **O**n **M**onday?' – practical ideas is what we need, suggestions for what to do, and how to evidence what we're doing, rather than complaints that we're not doing enough.

This series is a collection of ideas that will help teachers to deliver on those invisible elements of teaching and learning *at the same time as* teaching the knowledge and information required to pass those all-too-visible examinations. It is not either/or, it's *and*. We can continue to teach to a syllabus but we can do it in ways that do not stamp out those qualities that our charges will need when they eventually leave us; qualities that I believe all children have by virtue of being *human*.

I hope these books will shed some light on the invisible elements of school life – those human aspects that are seemingly immeasurable and difficult to report on, but no less important in the world outside school: our character, curiosity, creativity and our intrinsic motivation; the way we think; the way we communicate with each other; how we work together and depend on others to succeed.

These invisible elements are important *inside* school too. In fact, I believe they are essential if the child is to reach his or her academic potential whilst preserving their emotional well-being and self-esteem. Schooling can be an arduous voyage, and it requires far more than academic competence to stay afloat.

I don't believe one can separate the visible curriculum from the invisible one; they are interconnected and interdependent. Which is why, pleasingly, words like *attitude*, *curiosity*, *values*, *behaviour* and *relationship*s all feature in the DfE's *Teachers' Standards* alongside a requirement for demonstrating good subject and curriculum knowledge.

Let me give you an example: my son's Science grade again.

When he returned home recently with his end of term report, my wife and I were thrilled to see an A grade for Science. But it left me with some questions. Why was Henry performing better in Science than in Mathematics? Or Geography?

What is it about Science that means Henry is able to achieve such a high grade? It would be so easy to answer this question with a simple, 'Because he's better at Science than he is at Mathematics', or 'Because he enjoys it more.'

Why? Why is that?

The truth is there are so many possible reasons why Henry achieved top marks in Science, and almost all of them are invisible to the naked eye:

- he likes the teacher and is motivated to work hard for him;
- he dislikes the teacher and thought he'd 'show him':
- he sits next to his best friend in science lessons and feels happy and included;
- his science lessons are in the morning, when he is fresh and alert;
- he has science lessons in the afternoon and has usually woken up by then;
- his science teacher has a strict routine and Henry likes to know what to expect on a given day;
- his science teacher is unpredictable and my son enjoys the thrill of not knowing what will happen next;
- his teacher allows pupils to work together in groups, which my son enjoys;
- his teacher never allows group work and Henry prefers it that way as he likes working by himself without distractions from others;
- the science teacher likes to be creative in his style of teaching and allows Henry to be creative too.

And so on. You get the picture. Or rather, none of us get the picture of Henry through his science grades alone, whether they are for effort or academic attainment. These are only the visible signs, the results, of placing Henry in that subject, with that teacher, on certain days, in a certain room, at this particular stage in his life.

His teachers may choose to interpret Henry's grades as a sure sign that he is a scientist in the making, but that cuts both ways. If they dip will they look elsewhere for career ideas? Is it true, then, to say that because his French grade was lower, Henry is not a linguist or interpreter in the making?

No. Just as there are myriad factors contributing to Henry's current prosperity in Science, there are myriad reasons why he is not achieving the same levels in Geography. And, again, so many of these are *invisible*.

To divorce the visible signs of success from the invisible factors that contribute towards that success, beyond children's ability to receive, retain and regurgitate (the visible signs of 'work') is like telling a top tennis player, 'Hit the ball like that and you will always win.' As any sports coach will tell you, much of the game is in the head; it's there that the real battles are fought and won. Sports psychology is big business.

And as any good teacher will tell you, it's not just a child's ability to receive, retain and regurgitate that will bring her success; rather it has everything to do with her character, her attitude, her curiosity, her motivation, and so on.

The child will need these invisible qualities like the pen in her hand needs ink.

So let's call it *invisible ink.*

The learning environment

Wholesale changes to the way children are schooled are not necessary, even if they were achievable, because we have all we need already: what we currently have is a group of humans existing together in a building everyday, called a school. And where humans exist together there will inevitably be opportunities to develop the skills, aptitudes and attitudes required for adult life. It's an invisible curriculum, and it's already being delivered every day in every school. It is not written down and perhaps it neither could or should be, at least in the same, structured and progressive way that we have come to expect from school curricula and assessment systems. But it does need to be evidenced, of course.

It is often said that the moment we recognise the importance of something in schools we turn it into a subject on the timetable and immediately write a curriculum for it, accompanied by those all-important assessment criteria and level descriptors, of course.

None of the books in this series are proposing such action. Rather, I am arguing that we should indeed resist such temptations.

In saying so, this is not to say that any of the elements in an invisible curriculum *cannot* be taught or cannot be written down at all. The question is often debated isn't it: can character be taught? Can you teach someone to be curious? Is it ever actually possible to motivate someone else? Can someone be taught to be imaginative enough to create something original and of value?

The answer to all of these questions is a resounding 'yes'.

But such an affirmation comes with a caveat: one cannot teach character, or curiosity, or creativity – or any of the constituents that make up our 'invisible ink'

– from a rigid, incremental curriculum and through timetabled, discrete lessons. The rush to shoehorn in an extra half-hour period of 'character education' into an already cluttered and compartmentalised timetable needs to be resisted. Something quite different is required. A different approach. But it's not difficult, and it's not new. It requires no written syllabus. In fact such an approach is not based on any form of established, written curriculum. It is transferable across all subjects. It is dynamic, adaptable and entirely open to the kind differentiation of which learning support coordinators and gifted and talented officers could only dream.

It is called *you*.

This series places the baton firmly in the hand of the teacher. Whether you know it (or like it) or not, you will already be conducting the children's attitudes, emotions, ambitions, motivations and creativities: through the actions and attitudes and behaviours you model; through the things you say and the things you don't say; from the eye rolling or the subtle tutting to the great, big beaming smiles; from the way you plough doggedly through the piles of books on your desk, to the way you bounce energetically around the classroom, chivvying or challenging.

The climate of the classroom is yours to control. You are the thermostat. If you thought you were there just to teach your subject, you're in for a rude awakening. (No teacher I've ever met has ever believed this, I'm sure).

This series will not offer you a neatly presented, compartmentalised curriculum with separate schemes of work for each year group. Neither will it offer specific assessment criteria; there are no level descriptors in this book.

What it will do, I hope, is demonstrate how to create the right environment in which children's invisible ink can flow. It will shed light on that which can often become invisible – and falsely regarded as less important – in the rush to teach the visible things and pass the visible exams to reach the required attainment levels.

In so doing, this series will help you to *raise academic standards*. It will do this by focusing on six key features of the learning environment – an environment for which *you* are chief architect and in which *you* can make the greatest difference to the children's character, curiosity, creativity, motivation, communication, cognition and collaboration – their invisible ink. There are many features of an effective learning environment, but I should like to focus on six in particular throughout this series, and these are:

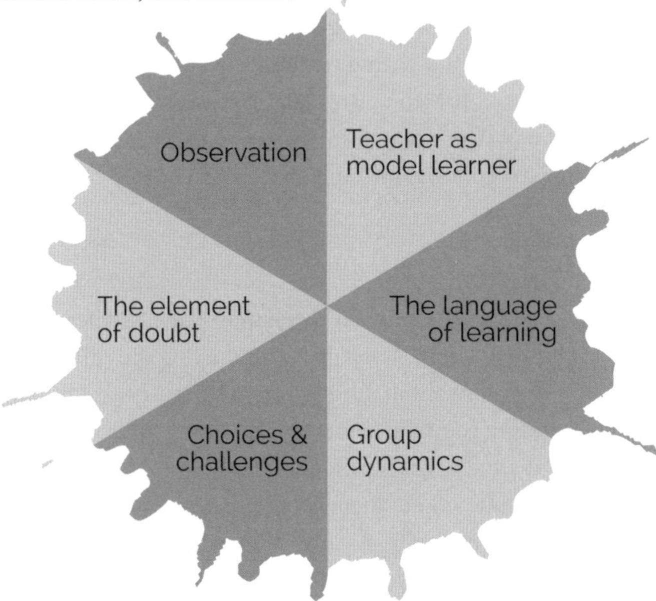

Figure 1: Six key features of the learning environment

Every title in this series includes chapters on each of these six features. Every aspect of the invisible curriculum, from character to curiosity to creativity and so on, will be viewed through these six lenses.

Can you teach character in schools? Can you teach curiosity? I believe we can *nurture* these invisible elements if we construct the right environment. The six key features of the learning environment which I offer are each built on a core belief:

1. As teacher, your own character traits and attitudes are being *modelled* all the time – just as your own interpersonal and communication skills are being mimicked. In the invisible curriculum, *you* are the model learner.

2. If we want to monitor and report on the children's invisible ink, we need to consider the *language* with which we do it. A new script is required.

3. *Group dynamics*, shaping the social environment in which you teach, have significant impact on how effective the 'invisible' learning will be.

4. *Choices* are an essential feature of the learning environment – moments of independence when children's attitudes are revealed by the decisions they make. They need the chance to opt in, or out, and to consider the consequences of choices made. Similarly, they need *challenges* and problems to solve, which will encourage their invisible ink to flow when they need it most.

5. There has to be the element of *doubt* in teaching and learning; that is to say, when we present knowledge, skills and concepts to the children in ways that are indubitable, beyond doubt, then we are shutting off their innate capacity to wonder, question, scrutinise and discover truths for themselves. Not only this, we are giving children the false impression that everything in life is certain, but it's not: established theories are being refuted all the time, historical assumptions can be questioned and commonly-held views are often at the mercy of subjective interpretation. This is how we evolve.

6. A fundamental shift from assessment to *observation* is required and an awareness of what is observable – what we mean by 'progress' and how we can evidence it as the child develops through school.

Addressing these six features of the learning environment will provide us with the insight, skills and tools we need in order to see the invisible curriculum at work, the right pedagogies and practices to deliver it and the language with which we can truly monitor the children's 'invisible ink'.

2 Perspectives: Teaching for character

Invisible ink flows through every good school, often celebrated but rarely monitored closely. But it is this lifeblood, this energy, that will determine the quality of a child's experience in school and the success she will find in adulthood.

Of the seven elements I have suggested which make up the invisible curriculum, there is a specific reason why I begin this series with *Character.*

In chapter one, I offered three historical assumptions about the purpose of education which I suggest have shaped the system of formal schooling that we have inherited. Those assumptions again, are:

1. The most effective way to bring about success for a society and its economy is to develop the *intelligence* of its younger generation.
2. The most accurate measure of intelligence, and therefore a predictor of future success, both for the individual and for the economy, is *academic qualification.*
3. The best way to incentivise students to study for academic qualifications is through a system of external *rewards and sanctions*, and the best way to chart their progress is by *examination*.

These assumptions have had some unintended consequences:

i. They have led to the slow erosion of children's natural *curiosity* and *creativity.*

ii. They have caused children's intrinsic *motivation* to be replaced by extrinsic motivators, as they respond to the rewards and sanctions on which school is built.

iii. They have led to a significant narrowing in how we view intelligence and how we value specific types of *thinking* over all others.

iv. They have restricted children's opportunities, and willingness, to engage in two-way *communication*, required as they are for much of the time to listen to or read an authoritative monologue instead. They have, to a degree, removed the notion of doubt, thus reducing the need for debate, discussion and questioning.

v. They have led to a diminishing of children's appreciation of the need to collaborate with others, and of how life outside school is built on *interdependence*.

The following six books in this series will address each of these unintended consequences, and provide ideas and strategies to redress the balance, resisting the temptation to provide a structure for measuring and grading such elements, but rather building the right *environment* in which those invisible elements can flourish, focusing on the six key features listed above.

But there is a further unintended consequence, and it is the overriding reason why these invisible areas of child development are so vulnerable to the 'side-effects' of a formal education: it is because the learning environment created by these historical assumptions may have a detrimental effect on children's natural character development. Formal education as we know it, shaped by these assumptions about its purpose, may be non-conducive to the development of the very character traits and attitudes needed to succeed – in work, in marriage, in friendship: character traits like grit, perseverance, empathy and so on. I've often wondered, an A grade in Mathematics is all well and good, but how does it help you with your marriage?

I believe it is *character* that we must address first, because it is a child's character traits and attitudes to learning that will determine whether her invisible qualities flourish or flounder in the formal school environment. It is character that will determine the degree to which a child remains curious or creative or self-motivated through school; it is character that impacts greatly on her willingness to communicate and collaborate with others; and it is character that will affect how and when and what she thinks. As Erik Jensen so succinctly puts it, 'How we feel is what's real; it's the link to what we think.'

In school, we can often see what children think in response to what we teach them, or at least what they 'know', or can remember, in relation to the curriculum because we ask them to write it down and then we attach a mark to it. But how they *feel*? This is less visible and is not subject to grade or value judgement, mercifully, though it is absolutely imperative that we monitor it. The emotional well-being of children is inextricably linked to the development of character. Low self-esteem, anxiety, these things are so very corrosive in the young – as they are in any of us.

Erik Jensen's insightful comment is especially relevant to us today, when we so often read of the tragic consequences of a system that is not designed to manage the children's emotional development as comprehensively as their academic attainment. Mental health in children is of supreme importance and it shows no real signs of getting any better. The pressure of examinations hangs like the sword of Damocles over children's heads, bringing immeasurable pressure and great expectation.

When you think about it, how is it that we prepare children academically for examinations without preparing them emotionally for the pressure of those examinations? This may be unfair – many schools do, I am sure, but in addition to the curriculum taught, as an adjunct, rather than *through* it.

Some schools prepare their children very well for the stresses and strains of coping with summative assessment. But not all, and if one studies the National Curriculum, or any other academic curriculum, taken as the canon of academic knowledge to be taught in school, one would be hard pressed to find many references to emotional intelligence or the character traits and attitudes needed to fortify the children in readiness for the expectations which we, and their parents, have for them, never mind the expectations that will await them in adulthood.

It's like training an athlete for a marathon by improving their fitness levels in a gym without ever venturing outside, or meeting other runners or encountering the weather or enduring blisters or getting tangled in other's people's feet.

Educators ignore these invisible elements of human development at their peril – or at the peril of those they are teaching.

In his excellent book, *The Restless School*, Roy Blatchford quotes the famous McNamara fallacy, a statement made by the then US Defence Secretary, Robert McNamara, to offer some explanation for what happened in Vietnam. Although the original context for the statement may have been war, it has been invoked in many situations since and is, I think, very relevant to us here.

> The first step is to measure whatever can be easily measured. This is okay as far as it goes. The second step is to disregard that which can't be measured or give it an arbitrary quantitative value. This is artificial and misleading. The third step is to presume that what can't be measured easily really isn't very important. This is blindness. The fourth step is to say that that which can't be easily measured really doesn't exist. (Blatchford, 2014: 34)

Let's take the example of a student, Katie. She is sixteen. It is predicted that she will achieve straight A* grades in her forthcoming GCSEs. Despite the predicted grades, Katie complains of feeling depressed and lacking self-esteem. The fallacy might follow: Katie is on line to achieve outstanding grades at GCSE. We can see evidence for this in the quality of her work and in the excellent results she achieved in the mock examinations. Such grades are an indication of an excellent performance in school and outstanding academic progress made. We do not have the same method for seeing the progress she is making emotionally. Thus we may even question why she is 'feeling down' at all when there is so much evidence to indicate she is doing so well. Her results are what counts and we put the depression down to 'just adolescence'. It'll go.

Such a hope that the invisible elements will 'just go' and the visible components, namely Katie's GCSE grades, are what will endure is naïve at best and seriously dangerous at worst.

A Headteacher will often say that his or her school offers 'a well-rounded education, in which character development and creativity are valued as highly as intellectual advancement. 'At our school, we educate the *whole* child.'

Quite right. It would be odd not to. I can't imagine a child with an educated head and a feral body or a particularly ignorant foot. Noble words, and exactly the kind of thing I, as a parent and teacher, like to hear. I agree with this philosophy entirely and, even though it seems rather obvious, I like to hear it vocalised precisely because I know they are talking about the child's invisible ink – the aptitudes and attitudes needed to function well. The whole child means the visible *and* the invisible parts. The mass *and* the energy.

But in response to this claim, one might say: OK, so if you value character development as much as academic development, please show me this. Show me some proof that the children's well-being matters to you. I've looked at your curriculum and I've seen your excellent academic grades. But character development? Can you show me some evidence that this is equally valued, and therefore is being as closely monitored, as your pupils' academic progress?'

I suspect I'd be greeted with a look of incredulity at best and offered words to the effect of: 'The added value that we give our children in terms of character development and well-being will be self-evident when you meet our pupils. They're delightful.'

Nice dodge. But I have immense sympathy with this comment. It matters to Heads that their staff support their pupils' well-being as well as their academic potential. Nothing is more important to most Heads I meet than the happiness of their pupils (even though their own performance as school leader may well be based not on the happiness levels of their pupils but on the grades they achieve).

But I'm bound to ask, more of the system than the Headteacher, 'So is this all of your pupils all of the time? Are they all delightful? And if they're not, do you know why they're not? Can I meet any of the children and find them in a healthy state of mind, their character brimming with confidence and resilience? Or is that just the two children I passed in the corridor who I assume have been asked to give me the guided tour?'

In this fictional dialogue, I am guessing the next retort might be along the familiar lines of: 'Well, you see, just because we value something does not necessarily mean we must measure it, Mr Hammond.'

At this juncture I would pause for the obligatory Einstein quote, 'As the great Albert Einstein once said, Mr Hammond, not everything that can be counted counts and not everything that counts can be counted.'

OK. Understood and agreed. But one cannot help but respond with, 'So, is your belief that character, like curiosity, creativity or motivation, cannot be measured based on your past efforts to try and measure it and then finding that you can't? Could you talk me through those attempts, perhaps?'

Hmm… I thought not.

As Roy Blatchford tells us:

> …a school can readily measure pupils' attendance or library borrowing rates or reading ages – fine. But what about resilience, self-esteem and happiness, all vital to a student's well-being and success? We need to think carefully about what is and is not possible to measure, and find ways to record and report meaningfully. (2014: 35)

If we want children to remain curious and creative through school, if we want them to engage in effective communication and collaboration with others, and if we want them to learn how to think, we must first address how we develop their *character* – or perhaps I should say, how we can build a learning environment most conducive to the development of their character. We must then address how we can monitor this character development in meaningful ways, and provide evidence that we are so doing. And it is unlikely that those meaningful ways will include the stamping of a 'B grade for Determination' across someone's forehead.

Performance traits or moral virtues?

It is important to note early on in this book what we mean by the word *character*, since the word has many connotations that make us think of morality, religion, culture, ethics and societal values and beliefs.

Every school promotes moral virtues that form the fabric of the school's ethos and culture. These may reflect the religious teachings of a particular faith, for example, or may simply be the moral standards or behaviour codes to be adhered to if the school is to be a safe and prosperous place in which to learn. *Treat others as you would wish to be treated yourself*, for example, may be one such principle that appears within such a code or set of school rules, and it is very obvious why this is important in a school, as in life.

So let us draw a distinction between *moral* character and what I shall term *performance* character. It is with the latter that this book is concerned – the character traits and attitudes that enable an individual to perform to their potential and to work collaboratively with others. Though some of these will necessarily overlap with the moral virtues enshrined within a school's code or rules – because such rules are as concerned with the individual as they are with the group – there is a specific focus for us here, namely one's *attitude* to learning.

By 'character' I do not mean the aforementioned moral virtues as laid down by society or faith, and reflected in the behaviour code of a school shaped by the society or religion that built it. A 'person of good character' is deemed to be someone who is morally upstanding, law-abiding, honest, charitable, tolerant and considerate. He or she is equipped with a moral compass and is unfettered by the ravages of selfishness and greed.

All important virtues, without question. And they can and must be taught in school, as in the home. But a book designed to demonstrate which moral virtues should or should not be taught in schools and how, would be very difficult to write, because, pleasingly, the world is made up of many different faiths and cultures and codes and practices. There may well be some absolute (rather than relative) truths or taboos – the aforementioned 'treat others as you would wish to be treated yourself' seems a reasonable one, as does honesty, charity and kindness – but this book is not about these. It is about the psychological traits that I believe are innate in all children and must be preserved and nurtured through school. There are many other books of this nature, written by far cleverer men and women than I, in which the moral virtues and codes most valued by different faiths and cultures are examined.

This book is about the *self*.

It's about how each individual can survive and thrive in school when we, as teachers, build the right environment for them. That is not to say this book is all about striving for independence from others. I fear we attach too much importance to this in schools today. We work hard to move the children on from dependence upon us and their parents to independence, without realising that the true goal is *interdependence* – this is how the world works, how it must work. But true interdependence and collaboration require a positive understanding of oneself first. As Stephen Covey says in the fifth of his *7 Habits of Highly Effective People*, 'Seek first to understand, then to be understood.' (Covey, 1989 : 235)

Neither do I mean 'character' as in our personality. It could be argued, and this is certainly a view to which I subscribe, that one's personality is forged within those early years of childhood and may reach a more permanent state in early adolescence, perhaps. For my own part, I am certain I have the same personality that I had at school. Despite being in my forties, place me in a room with my contemporaries now and I am the same Hammond (or Ham'n'eggs) that I was at the age of twelve, with the same little foibles, eccentricities and habits. It is only when I look in the mirror that I am forced to accept that I have aged. Inside, I have not, and I'm not sure my own view of myself has changed either, though the inevitable challenges and failures one encounters in adulthood may have led me to view myself less flatteringly these days.

But the character traits and attitudes that relate to performance rather than morality, or personality, are not so fixed, rather they are dynamic and vulnerable to influence and the environment around us. They can be taught and learned. And they can certainly be modelled by the teacher for others to follow (see next chapter).

It is our performance character that will have considerable impact on how we learn, how we grow and ultimately how we function in society. We know that schools must teach moral virtues, and they do, through assemblies, through tutor groups, through PSHE lessons, through behaviour policies and through the general dialogue that exists between a teacher and her pupils. This book is about performance character.

I should also like to draw a distinction between possessing the optimum character traits and attitudes to learning to help us reach our potential, and possessing or showing *maturity*. Again, this is quite a different thing.

Does building character mean growing up?

Our attempts to build character in children are often hijacked by an expectation that children need to 'grow up' in order to succeed. It seems to me we measure success in childhood against some concept of being adult. Why do we have to calibrate childhood in this way? I have always believed that a childhood overly dominated by the need to prepare for adulthood is likely to lead to an unfulfilling and unhappy adulthood, ironically. And yet, conversely, the secure and happy adulthood is one that is built on the strong foundations of a childhood largely free of any pressing need to 'grow up' and start preparing for adulthood too soon.

I was running some writing workshops in a school recently, situated in a busy part of the South East of England, standing within the boundaries of the M25, that blessed commuter belt, stretched around ten percent of the country's population. I was complimenting a Year 5 child on how quickly he had filled his page with writing and how he had settled into his work without fuss or bother. He was, as we teachers say, 'on task'. His reply surprised me:

'Well, you have to get on don't you? I mean, life's too short 'innit?'

He was ten years old.

One can only imagine the conversations between him and his parents who, for the best intentions, I am sure, suggested unequivocally that he remove his finger from his nostril, pull his proverbial socks up and get a move on with things.

The character development to which I am referring is not at all concerned with the kind of premature adultification that seems to be seeping into our schools and homes. Building character does not simply mean growing up. I am not in the habit of hurrying children through their childhood and stubbing out all evidence of childishness. (When have you ever heard the word 'childish' used as a compliment?).

When have you ever seen an adult skip down the road? Why? Why is that? Skipping is an efficient and healthy way to travel. Come to think of it, when have you ever seen a teenager skip down the road? It's childish, isn't it?

To that boy in the writing workshop, I wanted to retort, 'Don't worry. Life is *long*. But *childhood* is short, so enjoy it for as long as you can. With luck, you'll spend four fifths of your life as an adult (and most of that time will be spent hankering after the first fifth).

To conflate 'character development' with 'growing up' is to miss the point and will only heighten the malevolent effects of formal schooling that I have highlighted. Perhaps I come from the 'Just William' school of thinking, or schooling, but I am talking about that kind of courageous childhood in which the infant is not afraid to 'have a go', to be resourceful, to take risks and to be happily oblivious to the kinds of pressures often exerted by the anxious parent. The days of 'Hey Mum, I'm off out, I'll be back for tea' may be depicted in sepia these days, but it was often in these untrammelled moments of exploration that the most beneficial character traits and attitudes were forged. I am not alone in this view; more than three hundred years ago, empiricist philosopher, John Locke, wrote,

> Farther advantage may be made by a free liberty permitted to [children] in their recreations, that it will discover their natural tempers, show their inclinations and aptitudes, and thereby direct wise parents in the choice both of the course of life and employment they shall design them for... (Locke, 1693: 80)

It has all become a little clinical now, hasn't it, with some parents, though not all, of course, feeling the need to account for every waking moment of their offspring's weekend, what with swim squad and private tutors and drama school and music lessons and taekwondo and Sunday league sports. Some children have busier diaries than their parents.

I wonder how many of today's children are afforded such 'free liberty'? Perhaps it is due to their refreshing contrast to the structured nature of formal schooling that I find Locke's 'recreations' so appealing. My reading of this is that if children are given time to be children, their innate character traits and capacities may be better nurtured, rather than compromised or driven out of them in the race to adulthood, or in the over-diarized moments between schooldays. The natural rhythm of childhood is better left to beat by itself occasionally, without resetting the clock to a different tempo all the time.

I cannot write on the subject of resourcefulness in childhood and proudly unstructured summer hols without quoting from one of my favourite poets of the twentieth century, Stephen Spender. I hope you will allow me this short tangential 'tea break' from our task. In Spender's wistful and aptly-named *Lost Days*, a poem I recommend heartily to you, we find a little boy lying on the grass in the long summer hols:

'Then, when an hour was twenty hours, he lay
Drowned under grass.'

He studies the creatures down there in the minutest detail. In the closing couplet of the middle section, *Drowned under Grass,* the image of the little boy 'holding the earth' is delightful. His character, his curiosity, his joie de vie and his sheer sense of awe and wonder are heartening to us teachers. He has *time* to notice nature.

'He pressed his mouth against the rooted ground
Held in his arms, he felt the earth spin round.'

(Stephen Spender *Collected Poems 1928-1985*: 147)

This chap seems a far cry from the boy whom I met inside the M25, and to whom life seemed so short. I'm not sure how much time that boy has spent gazing at ants – perhaps it is not an efficient use of his time?

Does this mean we should all close our textbooks, take off our shoes and run onto the school playing field to look for creepy crawlies?

Enormously tempting, but perhaps not everyday. To me, it means we should pause from time to time to consider how much 'free liberty' of the kind Locke called for three centuries ago, is permitted to children now – and the unintended side effects that such a lack of free time may be having on their innate character development.

When I was a Head, I would often proudly say to prospective parents, 'Here, education means muddy knees and a frog in your pocket.' Such a claim was shorthand for celebrating character, courage, resourcefulness and that insatiable, fidgety curiosity so synonymous with a proper childhood. What I meant, of course, was that we allowed the children time to explore, get dirty, delight in nature's wonders and enjoy some time to do what children do. And we recognised the benefits this brought to their character development and therefore their learning. I remember one prospective parent asking what the children did at break times if it rained. I looked at her somewhat surprised and said, 'They put a coat on, what do you do?'

But such an educational philosophy is always vulnerable to exaggeration and caricature, of course. There will be those who question how having muddy knees or playing with frogs, or gazing at ants and hugging the earth all the time gets you through your Maths exam.

Building character need not mean shaking off childhood. It means having the courage to explore, discover, question, create and solve problems independently. If growing up means discerning what is worth doing from what isn't and learning how to manage your time productively, then perhaps we should delay it for as long as we can and celebrate the importance and the value of an untrammelled childhood?

A century after Locke wrote of permitting children free liberty to engage in recreations, that they may discover their natural character and attitudes, Rousseau, in his seminal work, *Emile or On Education*, wrote:

> The wisest men concentrate on what it is important for men to know without considering what children are in a condition to learn. They are always seeking the man in the child without thinking what he is before being a man.' (Rousseau 1762: 43)

Perhaps there is insufficient time in our formal education system to consider 'what [the child] is before being a man'. How much of what we do and what we say is predicated on some pressing need to adultify children? There will be much focus in this series on how children grow and develop and learn 'invisibly' and quite apart from the 'measured, visible progress' they achieve in school, as matched against the expectations and standards laid down by Rousseau's 'wisest men'.

As Piaget (1969) tells us, having to adapt to adult modes of thinking and learning may hinder the natural development of character and personality in a child:

> Obliged to adapt himself constantly to a social world of elders whose interests and rules remain external to him, and to a physical world which he understands only slightly, the child does not succeed as we adults do in satisfying the affective and even intellectual needs of his personality through these adaptations. It is indispensible to his affective and intellectual equilibrium, therefore, that he have available to him an area of activity whose motivation is not adaptation to reality but, on the contrary, assimilation of reality to the self, without coercions or sanctions.' (Piaget, 1969: 58)

I consider the 'affective and intellectual needs of [the child's] personality' to be the performance character traits and attitudes which allow his curiosity and creativity to flourish. As Piaget says, these are not best satisfied or developed through the child adapting to modes of behaviour or thought that are laid down by adults in the room – the coercions and sanctions of the formal classroom, where there are scant choices offered. Character is not best developed in this way, or within an education largely predicated on the development of academic attainment (back to those historical assumptions again).

So performance character, as opposed to moral character, refers to those traits and attitudes that will enable a child to hold onto her innate resourcefulness, her curiosity and her creativity. Just as a successful adulthood is built on a childhood free from the pressing need to become adult too soon, so character development discovered through 'play' can often bring greater benefits to work than the kind of character development forged in the working environment alone, ironically. In the latter, the child is subscribing to Rousseau's 'coercions or sanctions', whereas in the former she is developing her character at the right time and in the right way. There is more meaning and application for her here, as Dewey might say.

Of course, such a thesis – that there is a right time to teach children and there is a natural rhythm and flow to child development that must be reflected in our formal teaching and learning at school – is not without its critics. Such a child-centred, naturalist approach, promoted by the likes of Rousseau and in later years, Dewey, Bruner and Montessori, may be viewed as too progressive by some, but teaching the 'whole child', addressing their character, emotions and creative capacities as much as their academic intellect is hardly new. Aristotle said that, above all, schools should teach character.

Engaging in pedagogical debate is like steering a ship in a storm, or driving a car on ice: we are always in danger of over-steer. Pitching progressive, discovery learning against rote learning, or child-centric against knowledge-centric, or an authoritative, propositional approach against a dialogic one will only end in hackneyed, polarizing criticisms. 'Gradgrinds' see any form of liberal play as an anathema, as welcome in the knowledge-centric, didactic classroom as weeds in a pavement; and die-hard progressive educationalists may see any form of formal instruction as an affront to a child's individualism – the authoritative machine presiding over 'just another brick in the wall' as Pink Floyd wrote.

There have been too many polarizing battles of this kind and they serve little purpose because they inflate the arguments either side to the point of hyperbole and caricature. I do not believe that pupils are sitting straight-backed, listening to Mr Gradgrind deliver the curriculum 'at them' with a cane under his arm in today's classrooms, any more than I believe they are creeping barefooted through the woods to 'discover their own learning' everyday. There are times when the learning is teacher-led, and should be, and there are times when a more independent stance is beneficial to the children. A blending of didactic and dialogic teaching is where good practice lies – and the majority of teachers know this today. And there is *never* a time when knowledge is irrelevant or should not be taught. I do not subscribe to the myths, so eloquently exposed by Daisy Christodoulou in her polemical book, *Seven Myths*, that 'facts prevent understanding' or that 'teaching knowledge is indoctrination'. Factual knowledge still provides the intrigue, the fascination, the awe and wonder and the context in which creativity and independent thinking skills can be encouraged. But just as we are waking up to the possibility of different kinds of intelligence beyond verbal reasoning, so there are myriad kinds of knowledge beyond the kind delivered through an academic curriculum. In suggesting we should be delivering knowledge of self, knowledge of others, knowledge of character, creativity and thinking, does not mean to say that suddenly we no longer value mathematical, verbal, historical or scientific knowledge that still dominates our school textbooks.

But isn't the very fact that we use the term 'child-centred' in schools a poor indictment of where we have got to? How can we pitch knowledge-centric against child-centric! If a school is not child-centred, then what is it? A shoe shop? A factory? A botanical garden? Of course a school is built, and run, with children in mind and of course knowledge enjoys high currency in the curriculum taught in that school, but the fact that we have to use this phrase indicates, to me at least, how those historical assumptions on the purpose of school have created an environment which may appear as anything but child-centred. An environment very much designed with one end goal in mind – academic qualification.

Children must adapt and evolve in order to cope with the demands of school. And yet school should adapt and evolve to meet the learning styles and learning potentials of children, shouldn't it? Or at least there should be a middle ground somewhere.

And so the over-steering goes on, and the inflations of my argument will follow: so you want a school to be a crèche, essentially, yes? And knowledge is dead, is it? You want every school to be a place in which the children set the agenda, where they decide whether they want to learn or not on a particular day and there are none of the coercions or sanctions that concerned Piaget?

Yes, and if we could dispense with uniforms altogether, give ourselves fantasy names and learn to fly, we could call it Neverland.

Whether you are a supporter of the Gradgrindian methods of the nineteenth century or the liberal, progressive practices and pedagogies that inevitably followed a century later, it is hard to deny that in the battle between academic advancement and holistic, naturalist teaching, we all know who won. Academic rigour is everything. And it's so beautifully measurable and recordable and articulable. Any attempts to draw our attention away from the pursuit of academic knowledge are interpreted as intellectually inferior, lacking rigour and therefore doing a tremendous injustice to children's chances in later life. (Because they will need to know how to solve simultaneous equations much more than they will need to know how to sustain friendships, endure challenges, work with others in a team, or survive a divorce?).

The very phrase 'soft-skills' for example, suggests an inferior rank, just as the phrase 'character-building' is relegated to outside the classroom, in which 'intellectually challenging' reigns; just as the word 'creative' seems inferior to 'academic' – at least in formal school it appears that way, just look at the distribution of teaching time given to the academic subjects over the creative arts or sports or outdoor learning. How many scoops of curriculum time is dolloped out to Dance or Bushcraft or Nature Studies?

(I always find it ironic that the word 'academic' can be used to describe something that is not rooted in reality and thus may be irrelevant or disputable. Not so in schools!)

Even the phrase 'team-building' is often greeted with a cynical roll of the eyes or a chuckle from the back of the staff room.

'Will we have to take our shoes off?'

'Are balloons involved?'

Team-building, communicating effectively, showing grit and so on, these may be invisible but they are far from 'soft'. And they directly contribute to your GCSE in Mathematics, no question. The fact they are not on the traditional curriculum, at least not within a discrete subject, comes as a relief and yet is a concern too: a relief because I would not wish children to be studying a rigid programme for character development, only to find that they will receive a grade for their grit or their discernment. On the other hand, it is a concern too, since anything that is not inked into the curriculum and ensuing schemes of work always runs the risk of being neglected.

All the more reason to build a learning environment, in which every curriculum subject is taught, that is conducive to character development – this is very much what this book is about, and why the following chapters are devoted to addressing those six elements of the learning environment.

The character within

What is encouraging – and we need some words of encouragement after a rather disconsolate start to this chapter – is that the character traits and attitudes children need to succeed in adulthood, those upon which all other invisible elements of the learning curriculum depend, are already present in young children, perhaps by virtue of being human. They are innate.

Permit me a short anecdote to illustrate this point. It is a story I have adapted from a delicious tale told by Ken Robinson.

Let me introduce you to Mary. She is in Year 3. It is a cold and rainy day in school – a day when a small, but ominous phrase, scribbled on the white board outside the Head's office, can rob students and staff of their optimism: an 'in-day'.

A hapless teacher, whose job it is to patrol the corridors and classrooms during playtime, (rather than haul up in the cosy staff room with a mug of coffee and a chocolate digestive), enters a particularly lively Year 3 classroom. Dodging the flying Connect-4 discs and the Lego blocks, she walks towards a little girl, who is sitting by herself at a table in the corner, drawing intently.

'Good morning, Mary,' she says.

Mary eventually looks up and whispers 'Hullo.'

'What are you drawing?'

Mary doesn't answer at first, but eventually mutters without looking up, 'I'm drawing a picture of God, Miss.'

The teacher rocks on her feet, tuts and chuckles for a moment and then replies with a shaking head, 'Well, Mary. I'm afraid no one knows what God looks like.'

Mary thinks for a moment, chews her pencil then puts it down and looks straight up at the teacher, an incredulous expression etched on her face.

'Well, they will in a minute, Miss.'

Hold onto this story. Savor it. Mary is showing exactly the kind of character she needs in order to allow her curiosity and creativity to flourish. It didn't occur to Mary that she might get the picture 'wrong'. It didn't occur to her that there was a right or a wrong way of depicting God. She knew what God looked like and that was that. Her curiosity, her creativity and the motivation she had to draw the picture in the first place are entirely dependent upon her character, her attitude to life and learning. Her courage, her grit. Good on you, Mary.

Here, in this crowded classroom, with the rain hammering down outside, Mary is showing some spirit. And, if carefully preserved, that spirit will enable her curiosity and creativity to endure school, at least for now.

Mary is able to persevere with her drawing in the relative chaos of the classroom. And she is demonstrating some optimism, that the picture she will draw will be any good at all. She is showing some self-worth, in that she is willing and able to tell the teacher what her picture is going to be of – had she not believed in her artistic skills she would have been very quick to dismiss it as 'nothin' really, Miss,' I suspect.

Mary has self-control too– she is able to sit and finish her drawing without being distracted by others. And Mary is showing adaptability – she is able to get on and find something constructive to do in the difficult climate of a wet playtime. One might even say she has discernment too – choosing to do something worthwhile with her time and talents rather than not. This might only ever be revealed at these less-structured moments – Locke's 'recreations' – when independent choices need to be made. You might say they *have* to be made. Sat in a classroom at breaktime, you have to make a choice of some kind – either you opt in or you opt out, you play a game or you don't. You choose to speak to someone, or you choose not to. Even sitting doing nothing is a choice you have made. The only time you don't make any choice at all is when the lesson resumes and you are told to do something by the teacher. (And when exercising your right not to follow an instruction is never going to be acceptable).

Character traits and attitudes

In the story of Mary it is comforting to see those character traits and attitudes in flow. Without these qualities, I don't believe Mary would have drawn this picture – I don't believe she would have set down on paper what, according to the teacher, no one else has ever managed to do, draw a picture of what God looks like.

Contrast this then with the character shown by the teacher – whose character, it seems, has been shaped by the usual pressures and cynicisms of adulthood. Her immediate reaction is revealing isn't it. 'No one knows what God looks like', so why bother trying to draw it if there's every chance you'll get it wrong?

It is those historical assumptions at work again, creating a culture in which it's good to be right and bad to be wrong. School should be the very best place to make mistakes. But it's not – in some ways it may even be the worst place to get it wrong and the best place to get it right.

Contrast this too with Mary's character and attitude in the formal classroom once the bell sounds for the end of playtime. When the next lesson begins, the teacher will set the agenda and the teacher will prescribe the parameters in which Mary can either get it right or get it wrong once more. The success criteria will be made abundantly clear to her. Yes, of course, Mary's teacher may wish to tap into her creativity and spark her curiosity through good teaching. She may enjoy a caring and respectful relationship with her, nurturing her self-confidence and self-esteem. But she will do all this in the knowledge that soon she will have to show that Mary has made 'progress'; she will need to measure and record her attainment levels and she will need to show that Mary is on the road to achieving academic qualification. One cannot escape the inheritance left to us by those assumptions: it's good to be right, bad to be wrong when examinations come along. And since much of the teaching and learning in schools is in preparation for those examinations, then the mantra 'right-good, wrong-bad' prevails.

The unintended consequence of this is that, despite her teacher's best efforts, Mary may still lose her self-confidence; she may lose her grit and resilience to 'have a go', fearful that she may get it wrong. She will lose her self-control because the learning environment will be controlled for her, with rewards and sanctions in place to ensure she behaves herself. She will have no need for discernment – she will be told what is worth doing, worth knowing, and what is not. It is unlikely she will have to make such a choice. And her optimism may slowly dissipate when she finds that what she thinks is a good picture, or a good story, falls below the required standard, the expected grade.

No one, least of all Mary's teacher, I'm sure, would seek to deliberately rob Mary of the innate character traits and attitudes she needs to keep her curiosity and her creativity alive. But where in the formal classroom, and in the visible, established curriculum which so dominates it, is Mary's character being consciously and actively developed or monitored or reported on? Who is showing Mary how to build up her grit? Or her discernment? Or her optimism? Who is explaining what these are, and what they are for?

I believe the teacher is modelling them, either consciously or subconsciously.

In this book I will provide some suggestions for maintaining these character traits and attitudes, in a more conscious and pro-active way, by building a learning environment in which they can flourish – this, in my view, is better than pouring them into a scheme of work and teaching them discretely in a separate subject, divorced from anything else. Having a separate lesson called 'character education' is as absurd as learning how to be a good citizen only on a Thursday, period four, between English and Geography.

I remember in a school in which I taught some years ago, whenever a pastoral issue arose in the staff room and there was a problem, the Head would turn to the newly appointed PSHE Coordinator and say, 'Don't you cover this in PSHE?' She would reply, 'Yes, don't worry, we're down to do it next week actually,' at which point everyone else in the staff room would relax – not their problem any more.

For any character education to be successful, it requires a 'buy-in' from the whole staff. It needs to be built into the fabric of the school – into the learning environment in every classroom, and not simply left to the PSHE Coordinator to do. It's like saying that spelling and handwriting are the sole responsibility of the Head of English or Literacy Coordinator (a comment on which I have been on the receiving end more than once).

There are myriad character traits and attitudes that enable us to perform to the best of our ability in school. To list them all would be impossible, and may lead us into a debate on semantics anyway.

I have chosen seven, and I define them thus:

Grit	courage and tenacity in the face of adversity and the resolve to commit to long term aims
Adaptability	being able to embrace uncertainty and adapt and modify to accommodate change
Optimism	the ability to respond positively to negative criticism and 'bad news'

Self-control	being able to regulate our emotional responses to the actions and conditions around us – we cannot control circumstances or others' actions, but we can control our reactions to them.
Empathy	an awareness and understanding of others' feelings and needs
Discernment	being able to distinguish between fact and opinion; knowing that what is happening and what **we think** is happening may differ, depending on how we see things and how we feel at the time.
Trust (Participativeness)	understanding that we all depend on others in one way or another; recognising the benefits of trusting and being trusted within a team.

Figure 2: The character traits and attitudes for optimum learning performance

For ease of reading, let us call these seven character traits and attitudes 'CTAs'. Readers may wish to add more, of course. We are, after all, infinitely complex mammals. But this book is not infinite. And seven is better than none.

CTA 1: Grit

There has been much written and discussed on the subject of grit in recent years; it has become a popular word in education. It has, I think, become shorthand for many other terms and phrases such as determination, courage, tenacity, perseverance, commitment and so on. Our grit is like a tea bag – its strength can only be measured when we are placed in hot water. But it *can* be encouraged to develop without making life difficult for students all of the time.

Deliberately placing children in challenging situations in order to observe and measure their levels of grit seems harsh. But we must resist the usual over-steer here. I am not advocating that we raise all children in the school of hard knocks – finding fiendish ways in which we can make their childhood as difficult as possible in order to 'toughen them up' and build their character. Very often, activities that are sold to children as 'character-building' can be soul-destroying in the end and do little for their self-esteem or self-confidence; it's a risky business.

But children do need to experience failure and learn how to manage it. They need to learn how to manage anxiety and fear. They need to be given the opportunity to show commitment to long-term goals. If we shield them from these experiences, if we protect them from all potential failures, then we are doing them great harm. But we need to take such care here. It is well known that anxiety and fear cause untold damage to children's brains, especially in the early years of childhood. Too much exposure to scary or stressful circumstances can lead to 'synaptic pruning' (loss of brain cells) when the brain uses up glucose to deal with stress that would otherwise be used to develop brain function and build connections.

But I am not suggesting that any attempt to place children in situations in which they need to show grit must be devoid of any support or understanding. At the risk of repeating a mantra too often, it is not 'either/or', it is 'and'. You can challenge and stretch children, provide moments for them to show grit, at the same time as giving them lots of encouragement, love and support. Challenging does not mean neglecting.

But I am also a strong advocate of the teacher exemplifying those CTAs for the children to follow, and in the next chapter I highlight examples of when teachers are showing their grit. You may be surprised how often we do this on a day-to-day basis.

When considering the importance of grit, and the benefits to be found in monitoring children's development of this character trait, we can find much insight from Angela Duckworth's interesting work with military cadets in the US.

After leaving her job as a management consultant, Duckworth began teaching seventh graders in a New York school. She soon realised that IQ was by no means the only thing separating the students who were successful and those who were not. She found that some of her strongest performers did not have the highest IQ scores and some of her most academically gifted pupils struggled sometimes.

Keen to know why those with the highest IQs did not always outperform others at her school, Duckworth re-trained as a psychologist. She then worked with a number of different institutions to consider what other predictors of success might be observable. Her work with West Point Military Academy has been particularly well-documented, in which she devised a survey known as the Grit Scale, in which she was able to predict the cadets most likely to stay the distance.

But Duckworth did not only work with young adults striving for a career in the armed forces, where the need for grit is obvious: she worked with students in the National Spelling Bee, with teachers from a range of different schools, and with sales employees in companies, each time looking for any common character traits shared by the strongest, most successful performers.

Across these quite different contexts, she found that the most accurate predictor of success was not IQ, social intelligence, good looks or physical health, but *grit*, which Duckworth defines as passion and perseverance to commit to long-term goals.

Duckworth then worked with thousands of high school students in numerous schools, giving each of them a questionnaire designed to reveal their character traits. Despite questioning the students on many different character traits and also considering other significant factors like socio-economic background and parental support, Duckworth found that the one character trait shared by all who went on to achieve success was *grit*.

According to Duckworth, the single best way to support children's grit is by instilling in them a *growth mindset* – a belief that the ability to learn is not fixed.

This is a central theme which I shall keep coming back to across the Invisible Ink series.

In the following chapter I shall look at how the teacher can play a significant role in developing grit in the children, by modelling it herself and by demonstrating the same growth mindset which Duckworth, and many other educational psychologists like her, believe to be so important.

CTA 2: Adaptability

I genuinely believe that most children want to know 'where to hang their cap' in school. They want to feel there is a place for them – that they exist. This is why, especially in the early years, the individual names and pictures that can be found above the pegs in the cloakroom or classroom are so cherished.

Similarly, older children need to feel there is a locker or a desk drawer for them. It is their own space and, for many, the rock around which they tether themselves.

The ritual of placing your coat on your own peg, storing your books in your desk drawer or placing your sports bag in your own locker is important for many reasons of security, stability and identity during what can often be a frenetic and demanding school day. It is little routines like this, especially at the beginning of the day when children must say goodbye to their parents, that help to reduce anxiety for many pupils. But this is not to say that routine is king. If we carefully stage manage the entire school day, every day, every week, we run the risk of removing any opportunities children have to learn to be adaptable – and this, I believe, is a very important character trait indeed.

The ability to embrace uncertainty and adapt and modify to accommodate change is a significant life skill. But the structure of a school timetable mitigates against any uncertainty. It schedules lessons, run by the clock, and allocates rooms. It tells children who will be teaching them, where and when. With the fashion these days for learning objectives to be written boldly on the board and discussed at the beginning of every lesson, children know what to expect in most lessons too.

I recall one school in which I took over from a previous Head of English. In the first lesson the Year 7s entered all carrying the same orange books. 'I'm glad you've brought your books,' I began, cheerfully, 'We're going to do some story-writing today.'

They looked at me incredulously and one piped up, 'These are comprehension books, sir, it's Monday. Story-writing is on a Thursday.' Needless to say that rule didn't last long.

Though many of us might agree that adaptability is an important character trait, it is hard to see how it is truly developed in such a structured and certain environment.

In Michael Gelb's excellent book, *How to think like Leonardo Da Vinci,* he suggests seven Da Vincian principles – character traits, attitudes and skills that will help a person to find success and unlock their creative potential:

Curiosità – An insatiably curious approach to life and an unrelenting quest for continuous learning.

Dimostrazione – A commitment to test knowledge through experience, persistence, and a willingness to learn from mistakes.

Sensazione – The continual refinement of the senses, especially sight, as the means to enliven experience.

Sfumato (literally 'Going up in smoke') – A willingness to embrace ambiguity, paradox, and uncertainty.

Arte/Scienza – The development of the balance between science and art, logic and imagination. 'Whole brain' thinking.

Corporalita – The cultivation of grace, ambidexterity, fitness and poise.

Connessione – A recognition of an appreciation for the interconnectedness of all things and phenomena. Systems thinking.

(Gelb, 1998: 9)

Any one of these principles is of great significance to this series, since they are all key constituents of the invisible curriculum and I shall be returning to Gelb's Da Vincian principles several times throughout this series. For now though, I should like to focus briefly on *Sfumato.*

According to Gelb, Sfumato is the most valuable of all the principles, since many of the creative geniuses in history seem to have possessed this in much greater quantity than their peers. Certainly the ability to embrace, rather than be fearful of, uncertainty is a key characteristic of successful people and an integral part of the creative process.

Life is far less predictable than school seems to suggest. The ability to adapt to change and to embrace uncertainty is a significant predictor of success and a characteristic much in demand in a world that is experiencing such a rapid rate of change. As Gelb tells us:

> In the past, a high tolerance for uncertainty was a quality to be found only in great geniuses like Leonardo. As change accelerates, we now find that ambiguity multiplies, and illusions of certainty become more difficult to maintain. The ability to thrive with ambiguity must become part of our everyday lives. Poise in the face of paradox is a key not only to effectiveness, but to sanity in a rapidly changing world. (Gelb, 1998: 150)

Counter to this, of course, is the notion that children learn best when they feel comfortable and safe; when they know where to hang their aforementioned cap. So I am not suggesting that school should be an unsettling experience, filled with deep uncertainty and ambiguity. But learning to respond to change with courage and optimism will be of huge importance in adulthood. And besides, it's fun to ring the changes now and again.

There are opportunities to observe this CTA in action even in the most regimented school: at the beginning of each academic year, for example, there is plenty of change and unfamiliarity around. At the beginning of a new topic in class there is uncertainty too. At the point when an exam paper is opened there is plenty of trepidation, I'm sure. But who is currently observing this in the children at these or other times? And where is the script with which to do so? Is adaptability discussed much in schools? Where does it feature in the curriculum? Could we find opportunities to remind the children how adaptable they have already become from time to time. And, as we'll see in the next chapter, could we as teachers demonstrate this adaptability to our pupils?

I might go even further and argue that embracing uncertainty and feeling quite comfortable with a certain amount of disorder is positively discouraged in school and there are penalties for creative souls who are not motivated by routine and regularity. I was constantly chastised when I was in schools for not knowing which lesson came next on the timetable or pitching up at the wrong classroom occasionally; it was the same when I was a pupil too.

Mixing up the routine from time to time, teaching in less predictable ways and surprising the children with unexpected challenges now and again are, I believe, excellent ways of encouraging adaptability and I will discuss these in more detail in the chapters that follow.

CTA 3: Optimism

In his book, *Learned Optimism*, Martin Seligman (2006) suggests that optimism is key to the learning process. He tells us that it is the way in which students 'explain' their bad grades to themselves that is crucial. He believes that for many pessimistic students, such self-explanatory patterns are permanent, personal and pervasive. So he calls them the '3Ps'. Such patterns can and do have a profound effect on children's performance in school and beyond. Optimism can be learned.

Conversely, Seligman tells us that pessimism and helplessness can be learned too, and it is this that can be so corrosive to a person's character and well-being. Seligman's and Steve Maier's studies of learned helplessness, though unpopular with behaviourists schooled in Freudian psychology at the time, proved that learned helplessness or optimism is concerned more with self-explanatory patterns than some instinctive motor response to external rewards or sanctions. 'We thought the behaviourist notion that it all comes down to rewards and punishments that strengthen associations was utter nonsense.' (Seligman, 2006: 24)

Paul Tough phrases it succinctly for us, in his superb *How Children Succeed,*

> Failed a test? It's not because you didn't prepare well; it's because you're stupid. (2012: 54)

...'Why didn't you do your homework?' could easily be interpreted as meaning 'What's wrong with you? You can't do anything right!'.

I don't think this is far-fetched; as a teacher and parent myself, it sounds quite plausible. Perhaps all of us harbor a propensity for negative thinking – it would explain the huge popularity of cognitive behaviour therapy books and websites. One might say it is a design fault for most humans. Children often take constructive criticism very badly, don't they, and this can so often lead to feelings of helplessness – when they feel they cannot help themselves to get better. They are no longer in control so what's the point in trying?

Whilst delivering INSET in schools, I have often indicated that as teachers we are cognitive behaviour therapists to our students. Optimism is a crucial tool in our kitbag for life, not only for success in school but in adulthood beyond. One might call it 'tough optimism' – that is to say not just an optimism that helps us to 'always look on the bright side of life' as Monty Python sang, or to dance Eric Morecombe like about the corridors singing 'Bring me Sunshine' (though it still remains my favourite song and should be introduced as a school hymn in every institution). Tough optimism means to deliberately and strategically explain criticism to ourselves in ways that are not so permanent, personal or pervasive. It is not just a 'sunny disposition' it is a survival instinct and a learned strategy to protect us from pessimism and helplessness. This is a very difficult thing for adults to master, never mind children. Where and when are we currently teaching this in school? Or observing, assessing and reporting on it? When do we talk to the children about pessimism and optimism and the consequences of having each?

It's taken me forty-three years to realise that no one is physically capable of making me miserable; the only person who can do that is me. Why didn't anyone tell me this at school? Why didn't my teachers tell me that the way I explain poor results or bad news to myself is what matters most? Why wasn't I told that no one can actually upset me, it's just a matter of controlling my response to upsetting remarks – and only I am fully control of that.

Where, in the predicted levels and grades we give to students, are we including their learned optimism (or pessimism) and the significant effect this will have on the progress they make? It's invisible, so we ignore it.

If a child's academic attainment levels slip from an A to a C, only then might a school consider the reasons for such a decline – although my guess is many schools will say it is because the child has not understood some element of the syllabus well enough (which may then be interpreted by the child and his parents to mean that he has reached his intellectual peak in that particular subject – back to the helplessness and pessimism again). But it is conceivable that, rather than intellectual capacity, a decline in academic achievement may be bound up with any number of their CTAs – and especially their *optimism*.

CTA 4: Self-control

It is difficult for children to develop self-control when so much of the environment around them is designed to remove the need for self-control – they behave themselves and there are clear rewards and sanctions in place to monitor this.

But self-control means more than not fidgeting in class, or not thumping your classmate when he whispers you're an idiot. Self-control, just like learned optimism, is about understanding that you can exercise control of your own actions and responses to people and places around you.

Sometimes we see children who resemble balls in a pin-ball machine, rattling around moving from one reaction to the next, with no discernable self-control or perspective. It's all too easy, especially when times are difficult and circumstances don't go our way, for a reactionary mode to become engrained within us and we become no better than a sofa – retaining the shape of the last person who sat on us, until the next one comes along. Self-control means having the grace and poise to reflect, accommodate and assimilate and keep a sense of perspective.

Self-regulation, self-directed learning, these are very valuable skills in the classroom and will enable children to take more ownership of their learning and betterment, and develop the understanding that *they* are masters of their own destinies. When children feel that they are not, that is when helplessness and a passive, fatalistic attitude kicks in. Seligman's explanatory style is relevant here:

> Learned helplessness is the giving-up reaction, the quitting response that follows from the belief that whatever you do doesn't matter. Explanatory style is the manner in which you habitually explain to yourself why events happen. It is the greatest modulator of learned helplessness. (Seligman, 2006: 15).

Teaching self-control enforces the notion that far from being helpless to change or improve or grow, children are in control.

Education must be about giving children a greater feeling of empowerment and a sense of their own identity. Self-actualisation is an end goal for all of us, and yet so many of us go through life without it, perhaps because it just never came up on the syllabus when we were at school.

It is worth noting that I have not included self-worth or self-esteem in the list of CTAs. I believe that these are the products of positive or negative character traits and attitudes, they are not CTAs in themselves. If a child has grit and self-control and optimism (able to respond positively to bad news and poor grades) then their self-esteem and self-worth will be necessarily higher. I don't believe one can teach self-esteem any more than one can teach a child to be happy, but one can develop the character traits and attitudes that will enable children to view themselves positively.

CTA 5: Empathy

The ability to empathise with another person, to see life through their eyes, to experience circumstances from their perspective, must surely be one of the most important milestones in a child's cognitive and social development. Preschool children are largely ego-centric, and necessarily so. For Piaget, in this 'preoperational stage' children think of everything only as it relates to themselves. The origins of this, for Piaget, lie in the earlier stage of infancy, what he termed the 'sensorimotor stage', in which, eventually, 'object permanence' occurs and the infant comes to realise that something other than himself can exist even when he can't see it.

Realising that objects, and people, exist quite apart from yourself is a pretty important thing to appreciate isn't it, and I can almost hear my teachers from the past reminding some of my more selfish classmates that 'other people do exist too, you know. It's not all about you.'

Moving from the sensorimotor stage to the preoperational stage, children are aware of what is around them, and separate from them, but their knowledge grows entirely through what they are experiencing rather than what they are told (a theory that has profound consequences for teachers one might suggest!). They gather information from what they actually experience and then overgeneralize.

Because children overgeneralize based on how they themselves view the world and experience it, this inevitably leads to the conclusion that everyone feels the same way they do; everyone sees the world in a similar fashion and everyone is motivated by the same drivers.

Perhaps this is why 'treat others as you yourself would wish to be treated' is such an effective school rule, to be found in just about every school I should imagine, in one guise or another. For preoperational children seeing is believing and they may find it hard to do anything other than to concentrate on the character traits and attributes of a person they see at the time, overgeneralizing that this is how they are, this defines them. To place the actions they see in others, or the words they hear spoken by others, into their proper context (i.e. to understand the reasons behind them), is difficult for young children. If they meet a man who is angry, then he is an angry man, as opposed to a happy man, who may have smiled at them once.

But if Dewey and Piaget's belief that children learn through experience rather than simply by being told, is correct, and I see no reason to doubt it, then this can be a very effective tool for teaching empathy. 'Put yourself in their shoes' is another phrase one often hears from teachers, seeking to draw some empathy from a child who has just said a hurtful thing to another. If children find it hard to imagine how someone else is feeling, they might find it easier to imagine how *they* would feel in their place. This seems pretty obvious, doesn't it

Empathy is such an important character trait to possess and it forms part of the canon of emotional intelligences we need in order in adulthood. For the teenager who is unable to empathise at all with others there are no boundaries, no taboos. The laws of a land, or the rules of a school, can regulate such a child's behaviour but one feels there is only one direction the child may eventually go – through the exit doors – because submitting to sanctions alone may not be sustainable if there is no empathy to highlight why we have rules in the first place.

If being in a school is indeed like living in a crowd, as Philip Jackson says, then understanding how others may feel is crucial. But I can't help but feel that this is rather like asking a job candidate to consider the thoughts and feelings of his fellow candidates as he enters a group interview. Or asking a jobbing actor to consider the hopes and fears of her fellow actors when entering a group audition.

The dominant system of monitoring and assessing progress in school sometimes resembles a group interview or audition, with everyone vying for top spot (or bottom spot if they're too cool for school). It's hard to empathise with others when you feel you have to do better than them if you want to win the academic prizes on speech day or the greatest number of housepoints.

'So, you're all competing against one another but you must empathise with one another too, please.' It's an odd dynamic, isn't it?

The truth is children are not competing against one another all of the time in school and every good teacher knows that 'personal bests' are the order of the day. But there will be some parents who are itching to know whereabouts their little Jake is in the class rankings and Jake will be all to aware of this, as will his teacher. Some students themselves will be very driven by reaching the podium and they may see little point in expending energy on empathy, unless there's an examination on it.

Using the six key features of the learning environment, empathy can be modelled for the children and it can be encouraged through the language we use, the choices and challenges we set, the group dynamics we establish for our class and the observations we make. Like all the CTAs, empathy is better developed this way than by teaching it from a curriculum and then stamping a grade on it.

CTA 6: Discernment

I've heard it said that there is more new knowledge contained in one edition of the Daily Telegraph than a person living two centuries ago would learn in their lifetime. It's somewhat difficult to prove that one, as it depends very much on the kind of knowledge we are talking about: interpersonal, intrapersonal, environmental, existential? Or are we referring to the highly-prized knowledge of what some clumsy politician has now gone and said, or what some errant celebrity has done in a public place and with whom? I suspect it's the latter, since this does seem to fill many of our newspapers these days, even the broadsheets, and it's unlikely that an early nineteenth century person would possess very much of such knowledge, or care to for that matter.

But the point is significant; we are indeed being bombarded by knowledge (or information?), edifying or not, from all quarters. The advent of the Internet has meant that, in theory, we can access just about any factual knowledge we care to wish to know at the click of a button, and an awful lot more that we don't. The tantalising prospect of a global brain is often mooted, and a global consciousness.

The much-peddled view that teachers are no longer the sole purveyors of propositional knowledge has led to the very role of a teacher to be questioned: 'Who needs teachers, all you need is Google?' No one actually believes this, I'm sure. The myriad lessons learned in the interaction between teacher and pupil extend far beyond the factual knowledge delivered, encompassing lessons in character, social skills and so on – knowledge of self and of others. As every good teacher knows, rapport is everything and when trust is established there is no limit to the value teachers bring to young minds, not least in learning how to learn, how to question and how to think.

But there is no question that factual knowledge can be accessed via means other than listening to the teacher. With such open access to all knowledge that has ever been recorded through a tablet or phone screen, and with the potential for anyone and everyone to upload as much knowledge as they download, there is a pressing need for *discernment*. It is not a question of knowing a lot, it's a question of knowing what is worth knowing and what isn't. The global encyclopedia is filled with as many pages of conjecture as it is with absolute truths, and children need to be taught how to discern fact from opinion, truth from lies or uneducated guesswork. You can download the complete works of Shakespeare as a free App these days. But discerning the lessons to be learned from the nine hundred thousand words that makeup his forty-three works is quite a different matter. It's not just about accessing the information, it's about discerning what it means and where it has come from (as I used to tell my students when they presented me with seventeen pages of printed-off Wikipedia text).

CTA7: Trust (Participativeness)

I've never much liked the old cliché, 'There's no 'i' in team'. I understand what it means – that there can be no single ego if a team is to function successfully together – and I entirely agree with it, but I don't like sound bites of this kind and I think they do little to inspire. After all, there's no 'we' in team either, though there are the ingredients needed for 'me'.

This CTA refers to something else.

I am referring to the child being open to the possibility of working with others, and understanding that if they collaborate they can achieve more. It is a mixture of leadership, followership, altruism, trust and the synergy that comes as a result.

The egocentric view of the world, with which Piaget was so concerned, and through which most infants gaze, is a necessary part of survival in the early years. Why should a baby share its milk? How can it even consider that another baby requires milk too?

The same egocentric view is seen in the early years at school – try asking two little boys to share a Lego set and you'll soon see the concept of collaboration is a tricky one to grasp. Dividing pleasure is as difficult as splitting Lego bricks.

But the world is built on interdependence, as I have said earlier. Being open to the idea of collaborating with others is an absolutely essential part of living and working in a group. A student can possess all the other CTAs in abundance, but if he is closed to the idea of working cooperatively with others than he is significantly limiting the success – and satisfaction – he may ultimately gain at school and beyond.

Some children are more collaborative than others, and so are some teachers. We have all worked with colleagues who are willing to share ideas and pool resources, and we may know others who struggle with this and see themselves in competition with colleagues rather than in union with them.

It is a question of trust – and this requires much careful attention to group dynamics, rules and values. I don't believe you can teach someone to trust you any more than you can teach someone to be loyal. But you can establish the right environment in which interpersonal trust can grow and individuals can come to appreciate the synergy, not to mention the enjoyment, to be found in working with others. This is how marriages, relationships, friendships and teams work. Without interpersonal trust any union will struggle.

Fortunately, we have the perfect conditions ready-made for encouraging this important CTA, in fact we have several in every school: a class, a year group, a team, a House.

Personalised teaching, differentiation, individual education plans and personal learning goals are all supremely important in a school, but so too is *teamwork* and that requires trust.

By 'trust' I am not referring to trustworthiness necessarily though it is obviously an important moral virtue. I am talking about participativeness – trusting in the group so that you feel it is worth participating, worth joining in. It is about knowing that together you can achieve more – knowing that we are all interdependent.

I struggled long and hard to name this seventh CTA. I wanted to call it *teamwork* or *collaboration*. But these qualities can only be developed from within a team – once its individual members see the benefit in pulling together. So this CTA is concerned with encouraging children to appreciate that working as part of a team is a good thing to do. It is indeed worth participating.

Whenever a group is formed, whether it is at school, home or at work, the success of the team requires a buy-in from the individual members and this means it *is* about me ultimately. It's about what I think of me and of others. It's about what's in it for me? Why should I join in? What are the risks involved if I do, and if I don't?

Children calculate these risks all the time and often they decide it is too risky to participate – the dangers of letting others down, not performing as well as others, being shown up, being made to feel useless, are all just too worrying and it's better to stand outside the team than stand within it, feeling unworthy or inferior.

The six key features of the learning environment will rescue us here. They will help us to show to children that they can trust others to welcome them and value them as they value themselves – that we are all in the same boat. By modelling trust herself, and showing how she works effectively as part of the team of staff, the teacher will encourage the child to trust in others too. Considering the group dynamics of the classroom has a very significant impact on the degree to which a child will participate, of course. The language we use when talking about teamwork is of great import, as are the observations we make when watching the children participate in the group. And, of course, the choices and challenges we place in the children's path will help us to highlight the real benefits of choosing to opt in, rather than opt out. So again, we can teach *trust* and *participativeness* just as we can teach the other CTAs if we consider the conditions in which they grow rather than how we are going to 'teach' them and when.

Six key features of learning the environment – a summary

My thesis, then, is that if a child is allowed/encouraged to continue to display these CTAs, then he or she will remain curious and creative and communicative through school. Lose any of these CTAs and the child will inevitably become less curious or less creative. How can a child vocalise their curiosity if they have no self-worth in class, or do not possess the courage needed to ask a question? How can the child dare to create something original if they do not possess the optimistic belief that it will ever be any good? Or if they do not possess the self-control needed to cope when the creative process throws up failures, as it will? Or the grit?

Or how will the child who possesses no empathy communicate or collaborate effectively with others?

It seems to me that we could do a lot worse than focus on these CTAs from the moment the child begins school, in the hope that if they are nurtured within him, then he will indeed become a curious, creative, motivated, thoughtful, communicative and collaborative learner.

All these qualities that make up the invisible ink, with which this series is concerned, require the right *learning environment,* which is built on those six cornerstones I featured in Figure 1 earlier, and which are:

- teacher as model learner
- the language of learning
- group dynamics
- choices & challenges
- the element of doubt
- observation

Let's begin with the first feature, teacher as model learner, and consider how we as teachers can model the CTAs for the children around us, since if we can show grit and self-worth and empathy ourselves, we stand a good chance of encouraging the children to do the same. This must be better than writing a discrete programme of study for 'Grit', chopping it into key stages, assigning level descriptors and then teaching and assessing it once a week, period 4 on a Thursday.

3 Teacher as model learner

A student following any subject in the visible curriculum accesses the knowledge and concepts that need to be learned (i.e. the syllabus) via a range of media: the good old-fashioned textbook, online research, learning videos and presentations, lectures, past examination papers and so on. It is visible. The syllabus is chopped up, placed in schemes of work, appropriately resourced and delivered.

The invisible curriculum is somewhat different, pleasingly. But there is a visible element to the development of character – a model which can indeed be seen and heard and imitated. And it's *you*, the teacher.

As I mentioned in the opening chapter, you are chief architect of the learning environment in which the children's CTAs are to flourish, and, whether you like it or not, *you* can make the greatest difference to the children's character development.

First things first. It is important to understand that the children like you. They love you in fact. There is something about you, something invisible, of course, that pleases them. There are many names for this – aura, warmth, charisma, enthusiasm, to name but a few. But my preferred word is *belief*. A teacher who believes in her pupils, and lets them know it, will earn their trust, their attention and their affection.

Think back to your own school days. Consider your favourite teacher, if you were lucky enough to have one. There may be several reasons why this teacher made such a positive impression on you, but I suspect one of the main reasons is that they believed in you. No matter how many times your messed up, either academically or socially, they still retained this dogged belief that you could and would amount to something more than you were at the time.

Now consider how much you wanted to be like them. It may have been their sense of humour that appealed most (it so often is); or it may have been their passion and enthusiasm for their subject; it may have been their ability to tell a good story; or it may have been the way they encouraged you with praise; it may have been their attention to detail – how they noticed even your smallest triumphs: finally spelling that tricky word correctly or managing to remember your entire eight times-table.

Wherever their gifts lay, it meant that you connected with them and, frankly, would probably have followed them over the top and into no-man's land if they'd asked you to.

What is interesting, when considering the rapport between teacher and student, is the way in which the student mimics the habits and practices of the teacher. It's an osmotic process. If you thought your favourite teacher was there just to teach the subject to you, think again. If you thought they just taught you Science or English or Maths, albeit very effectively, think again. They will have had a far greater impact on you than you may realise. They may have helped to shape your character traits and attitudes to learning, to others and to yourself. If your favourite teacher thought it was worth spending a bit of time working with you, then surely that meant you were worth something.

The best teachers I have ever worked with were always the ones who genuinely, wholeheartedly believed in the children they taught. They had a growth mindset, an optimism that was infectious.

But before we all treat ourselves to another viewing of *Goodbye Mr Chips*, *Dead Poet's Society*, or *Mister Holland's Opus* (my favourite film in this genre has always been Christophe Barratier's *Les Choristes*) it is worth reminding ourselves that such a positive and productive connection with children has huge responsibilities – because if they admire you enough to want to be like you, then they will mimic not only your good habits but your bad ones too. Nothing, nothing at all, will be as influential for many students as the mood of the teacher whom they admire most. To them, the teacher is the catalyst, the only one who can raise their hopes with a smile and a chivvying comment, or dash them with a look or a sarcastic word.

It is concerning how some teachers one meets don't seem to appreciate this. Perhaps this is precisely because they do not believe they have such a connection, they believe they are there to teach their subject, and will continue to do so, whether the children choose to listen or not. They've done their job and will collect their pay cheque. Perhaps such teachers are less influential and so it doesn't matter. But when that positive connection is made, when rapport is built, then the teacher can have such a significant impact on the quality and the quantity of the learning that takes place in her classroom. And nowhere is this more apposite than in the teaching and learning of the invisible curriculum, and especially in character development.

The trick is to be more conscious of the character traits and attitudes you are displaying to the children, so that you can display them even better, knowing that the children will pick these up by osmosis.

Let's take grit as an example. How and when do you show your grit? Such opportunities are not confined to the annual swimathon, when you amaze everyone by swimming further than anyone else on the staff. Or the staff fun-run, or the staff sack race on sports day. Grit can be shown in myriad ways other than through physical challenges (though cross-country runs are very obvious opportunities to model good grit for the children!).

In some schools I have visited, teachers commit to learning an instrument from scratch and performing their grade 1 piece in assembly at the end of term. This is an excellent way of showing grit. But there are simpler, more everyday moments when your grit is on show to the children. That giant pile of books on your desk that need marking – tell the children that by the time they return to school tomorrow morning every book will have been marked. You *will* do it!

The same can be said for any other of the seven CTAs I have listed. Take optimism for example. A 'can-do' attitude is so very important in school and you can be the catalyst for it in children simply by modelling it in your own work. If you are coaching a sports team, a heavy defeat to an opposing school presents the perfect opportunity to model optimism in the self-explanatory patterns you model – how you interpret and explain the defeat to yourself and others in ways that do not sentence the team to an entire season of disaster, but rather learn from it, build on it and become even stronger next time. Let's face it, victory is hardly the best way of gaining strength and resilience, only defeat can do that.

The same is true if you are managing a debating team, or taking a general knowledge quiz team for an inter-school quiz, or providing any kind of support when the children need to dig deep, face challenges and then face the even harder challenge of handling defeat. Tough, learned optimism is easily modelled for the children and they will imitate it if they see it in you.

Take another CTA, discernment. There are many ways in which you, the teacher, can model this character trait for the children, not least in how you spend your break times. Yes, of course, one needs to escape the classroom now and again for a coffee and a chocolate biscuit, but once in a while, if the weather is nice, why not sit on a bench in the playground and read a book? Or go for a walk around the nature garden or decide to do a litter pick or don a pair of wellingtons and weed the flowerbed. Any of these occupations model discernment because they show you are *choosing* to do something worthwhile with your time. There is nothing so influential over children's reading habits than seeing their favourite teacher reading a novel. And remember, you *are* their favourite teacher. Discernment means making the right choices and knowing what is worth doing or knowing and what is not. You will be making choices every day, perhaps without realising it, and these choices are being watched and imitated by the children.

Perhaps one of the CTAs most frequently modelled, and often unconsciously, is self-control. Managing your emotional responses to difficult situations in the classroom, moments that test one's patience particularly, is important for a myriad reasons, but from the perspective of teacher as model learner, it is crucial. When the difficult child persists in winding you up and taking great delight in refusing to do as he is told, the children will all be watching keenly to see how you react. Dig deep here. Resist the temptation to let others believe he has got under your skin. I have heard many a teacher shout at a pupil, 'Will you stop shouting, please!' How *you* manage stressful situations in class will largely dictate how the children will next time. How you react to the class bully will either serve to give credence to his role when you explode at him, or undermine it when you calmly take him to one side and ask him to return at breaktime.

I know a favourite question for many Headteachers when interviewing potential candidates for a teaching post is 'When was the last time you lost your temper?' Beware, this may be a bear trap, to which the only sensible answer is 'I don't lose my temper, it's safely guarded and only meted out in measured ways as the need arises.'

Showing evidence of being a model learner

The DfE's *Teachers' Standards* state that a teacher must:

> Demonstrate consistently the positive attitudes, values and behaviour which are expected of pupils. (DfE, 2011: 10).

This is proof of a recognition at government level that teachers themselves act as models for the behaviours they seek in their pupils.

If there is a requirement in your school to demonstrate evidence that you are meeting these standards, or even if there is not, it is worth considering how you can show that you are aware of your influence over the children as a model learner. It is worth spending some time compiling evidence to prove that you are showing the character traits and attitudes that you seek to develop in the children. This is achievable with a little thought and planning. The challenge is recognising the CTAs in yourself and remembering to make a note of the times when you have demonstrated them.

I have provided seven CTAs in this book. There are many more, of course, but showing evidence that you are demonstrating seven is better than showing no evidence at all. Consider how your character traits and attitudes are expressed at school and actively notice the opportunities there are to evidence each of them in a portfolio. In Figure 3 below, I offer some examples of evidence that you can include in such a portfolio, whether in note form, with a note of the date and situational context, or as photographic proof.

CTA	Evidence
Grit	learning a new instrument and passing Grade 1 or performing in assembly; competing in a sports event or charity fundraiser; completing a full set of reports; marking a full set of exam papers; planning and successfully managing a school trip or expedition; coping well with extreme weather conditions; battling on when mild illness strikes.

Adaptability	coping with a new classroom, new timetable or new role in September; covering lessons for colleagues; differentiating your teaching to meet pupils' needs; experiencing whole-school events when the timetable is departed from.
Optimism	motivating a school team to respond positively to a heavy defeat; mentoring pupils through difficult family circumstances or other forms of 'bad news'; introducing a new and difficult topic with a 'can-do' attitude and belief in the children's abilities; demonstrating a positive attitude via encouraging comments and positive feedback when marking.
Self-control	Carefully responding to instances of disruptive behaviour in class; Handling potentially stressful situations with colleagues; Managing moments of extreme workload calmly and in an organised manner; Responding professionally and calmly to difficult or unreasonable demands from parents; Showing restraint when your authority is challenged.

Empathy	Showing an understanding of parents' feelings and concerns over their children; Showing empathy for colleagues over work issues; Giving support to pupils – viewing learning objectives through their eyes and pre-empting worries; Marking work and writing reports in ways that show understanding of challenges faced and overcome.
Discernment	Choosing to spend 'free time' constructively at school, e.g. reading a book, gardening, rehearsing; Chairing a debating society or speaking club; Editing a school newspaper - demonstrating an ability to discern fact from opinion; Exercising good judgement in class, when responding to complaints and arbitrating pupils disputes; Applying classroom and school rules consistently.
Trust (Participativeness)	Participating in voluntary activities – school orchestra, clubs, staff teams and social events; Jointly planning lessons, events and trips; Participating in group assemblies and presentations; Coaching school teams and building synergy.

Figure 3: Evidence of teacher as model learner

4 The language of learning

If we are to create a learning environment that is conducive to the development of positive character traits and attitudes, then we need to address the language we use to facilitate and report on learning.

As I stated in Chapter 1, the word *progress*, for example, suggests advancement towards an established destination. This may work for the academic curriculum, which is fundamentally built on the final examinations and the levels of attainment one would expect from a child en route to those examinations.

But for the invisible curriculum, and especially for character development, who can say what the final destination is?

As I suggested earlier, the word 'development' implies growth from the root without indicating exactly where the destination is. There is no self-fulfilling prophecy here. No-one knows where it is heading, though obviously we can shape and guide such growth via the classroom rules and the school's behavioural codes and values. The word development promotes a growth mindset rather than a fixed one. The word progress, on the other hand, suggests there will always be a definitive end, a glass ceiling, perhaps.

Showing development in *grit,* for example, suggests that a child is learning to show great resilience and tenacity in response to challenges faced. She is learning to how greater resolve and commitment to long term aims. Conversely, showing progress in grit suggests to me that the pupils is progressing along an established line towards an acceptable or commendable level of grit. What is that exactly? Are they gritty all of the time in every situation? Have they reached a maximum level of grit, after which they cannot get grittier? Is the same true if we say someone has made excellent progress in empathy? Are they well on their way to an A grade in empathy? What do they need to do to get there? And how do they maintain their top level of empathy once they have been judged to have reached it?

When viewed through this lens, one can see the flaws in the language we sometimes use in school. Development does not suggest such a specific destination against which a child's progress can be measured, literally.

There are many other words which, though effective enough when monitoring and reporting on children's academic attainment, seem inadequate when commenting on their character traits and attitudes.

Assessment is one such word. Inevitably this suggests an inherent value judgement. Indeed, the word assessment can mean test – written assessment, controlled assessment, marked assessment, and so on. How then, if we regularly use the word assessment to mean test, which one can pass or fail, can we then use the word 'assess' when we are talking about monitoring children's character development? When we say assess do we mean *monitor*, see how something or someone is doing, or do we mean measure it, weigh it, take a reading for it.

Does the word *assessment* mean a test or does it mean the process of assessing? I think it is used in the former case more often than not – *an* assessment.

Within the context of the invisible curriculum, I would replace the word assessment with 'observation'. This cannot be confused with a test or any kind of value judgement being made. It means exactly what it says – *observe* the children, watch them, monitor them and record what you observe. You cannot sit an observation in the same way you sit an assessment, which means you cannot fail it. The observation is the teacher's to conduct, not the child's to pass or fail.

There will be much more on observation in the seventh chapter.

The word *results* may also be unhelpful at times when describing the children's character traits and attitudes too. Schools are often results-driven, though they may seek to reassure parents that this is not the case. But league tables don't help. Results are everything. This is true in life beyond school too, of course, where performance targets are agreed with employees and results must be reached. But again, within the context of the invisible curriculum, the word is misleading precisely because it is associated with something that is visible – a list of numbers or grades or percentages, which can be ranked and used to present the range of ability or attainment levels in a class. And how can we generate such a list of numbers for the children's levels of empathy or discernment? Or should we even?

The word *evidence* may be more helpful to us when commenting on the children's character traits and attitudes. At least this seems more open-ended and less numerical. Taken as a verb, how can we evidence the children's invisible ink? How can we demonstrate growth? There are myriad ways of doing this over and above the usual handwritten answers in a book or on an examination paper – but it depends very much on how we define another, hugely influential word in school – what we mean when we say the word *work*.

When preparing the neat piles of children's books on each desk in readiness for a parents' evening, I was often struck by how poorly these books had captured the excitement and engagement in learning that I knew was going on in the classroom. How little they showed of the energy and enthusiasm of the students, of their curiosity, their motivation and the character traits and attitudes that I knew were bringing them closer to being self-directed learners. None of this was evident in the books, or very little at least.

When I see my own children's books at school I am often reminded of the fields of Glastonbury the morning after the festival has ended. That is not to say at all that my children's books are messy and muddy (although I'm not sure about my youngest son's). What I mean here is that, reading through the pages, I get a sense that something exciting has happened but I have missed it. The scratchy, patchy handwriting and the half-finished drawings give a tantalising glimpse of a learning party going, like broken tents, empty beer cans and a mangled umbrella. I know that my son is enjoying his lessons – he often comes home brimming with enthusiasm and is so keen to tell me what he has learned. But rarely is this energy and active learning fully captured in his books because it takes him a while to write anything down. He doesn't really like fountain pens.

It is worth considering what we as teachers hear when we say the word 'work' in our staff meetings, and contrast this with what the children and their parents hear when you say the word 'work' to them.

I can illustrate this by recounting all those whizzy, interactive English lessons I tried to deliver, which often involved discussion and debates and role playing and poetry reciting. At the end of such a lesson the children would file out to break and I would so often hear someone pipe up, 'That was wicked, we didn't do any work… again!'

'Halt!' I would cry. 'Come back, please! You *have* been working. So why do you think you haven't been?'

'We didn't get out pens out, Sir, did we.'

I shudder at the number of times my pupils may have gone home and told their parents they hadn't done any work in English that day. And yet I do recognise the view that work in school involves a fountain pen or pencil and some paper with lines on it. It begins with the date and the title – underlined – and it ends with 'Right everyone, finish the sentence you're on, please, close your books and sit up straight.'

In this scenario, 'work' means showing results, doesn't it? Getting something into your book, so that you have visible proof that you did something today.

My guess is that many parents would agree with this. I have been on the receiving end when a concerned parent has booked an 'urgent meeting' with me and told me that her other twin daughter in the class next door seems to have much more in her book than the daughter in my class does. 'Why is that, Mr Hammond? Mary's sister seems to be doing more work than she does for some reason.'

However parents may view 'school work', even a cursory glance at the *Teachers' Standards* will show you that there is much one needs to be doing as a teacher over and above getting work into pupils' books! Promoting intellectual curiosity, a positive attitude and a love of learning is an important part of being a teacher, even if it does not always yield as much written work in the children's exercise books as dictation or copying from the board. But these broader teaching and learning aims need evidencing too.

In continuing our alternative lexicon, may I offer up the word 'learning' as a substitute for 'work'. This seems blindly obvious, so forgive me, but learning is what we want to see in school, isn't it? And we know as professionals that learning comes in many forms. Rather than thinking 'we need to get more work into their books to show progress and provide evidence of meeting the standards expected of us', should we not think 'we need to find ways of evidencing all the learning that's been going on.' And that means a range of media, including:

Talk books: recording insightful comments made and deep questions asked.
Speech bubble worksheets: A4 sheets with speech empty speech bubbles on, into which the children can write down some interesting comments that they either said or heard during the learning experience.
Photographs: taken during group discussions, drama sessions or other activities that may not always involve the use of a fountain pen.
Rolling images/videos of activities: displayed on the IWB, as parents visit for parents evenings and open days.
Mind maps or spidergrams: to record in a quick and efficient way insightful thoughts, plans and solutions to problems posed.
Timelines: of key facts learned, when they became known, discovered by whom and their impact today.
Word banks: glossarising important subject-specific words and phrases, which are discussed in class, and can be explained by the pupils.
Short plays and re-enactments: using drama to demonstrate evidence of knowledge and understanding in character and in context.
Scripted duologues: between two pupils, discussing what they have learned – written into pupils' books and/or performed on camera.

Figure 4: Creative ways to evidence active learning in the classroom, and beyond

These different forms of evidence for learning may reveal much more to us about the children's character development than hand written text in an exercise book ever could. The children's grit, their empathy, their trust in others and their self-control will all be more visible via such media as photographs and videos and insightful comments made and questions asked during learning activities.

So 'work' means learning, and that means gaining knowledge not only of the concepts, facts and skills bound up in the visible curriculum but knowledge of oneself and others too. By asking the right questions, and in the right way, we can find out more about children's adaptability or discernment or self control – and we can show evidence of growth in these areas in myriad ways. Of course, at the same time, we are showing evidence of how our own teaching is impacting on our students' learning and growth.

Another word which may not be helpful for the development of character traits and attitudes I have already alluded to earlier in the book – the word 'performance'. At least, it is unhelpful when the word is used in the wrong context, to mean something quit different. When we conflate performance with results we risk missing valuable opportunities to encourage, observe and talk about *how we learn.* When we say performance we must mean habits of mind, or learning habits, or the process of learning. Having the word 'process' in our minds when we say or hear the word 'performance' may help us to focus less on the destination (results) and more on the learning process. And this very definitely means considering the children's performance character – their CTAs.

Perhaps the most unhelpful word of all when considering children's character development in schools is the word 'ability'. Recent years have seen a move from ability to attainment, but one still hears it a great deal – even in the context of 'ability sets', which seems the very definition of a fixed mindset.

If the words *ability* or *attainment* dominate much of the learning experience in schools, then it's little wonder character development does not receive much airplay, since it cannot, and should not, be articulated in terms of ability or attainment levels.

But we do need some words to help us talk about the amount of grit or optimism that a child is showing, and how we, as teachers, are adding value.

'Capacity' might work, though this suggests a fixed mindset once again, since we are used to a machine, or a container, having a finite capacity. 'Potential' is a better word for us, though if we believe that all children have unlimited potential then it doesn't help at all if we want to comment on where the child's empathy is at a given point in time (not because we want to grade it, but we may wish to write about it). It is unhelpful to think one child's potential is greater than another's.

There is 'propensity', though that too suggests we will always expect them to show a certain level of grit or empathy – 'Jonathan has a natural propensity for...' or 'Lisa shows a tendency towards...'

It may not be a particularly attractive word that rolls of the tongue like attainment, but 'disposition' may work for us. When talking about their character traits and attitudes the word *disposition* allows us to comment on children's *current* empathy or discernment or optimism without suggesting that it is below or above par. The word is often used to describe someone's inherent qualities, after all. However, *disposition* can also refer to the way in which something is placed or fixed in relation to something else; a fixed mindset once again!

We may already have all we need with which to comment on children's CTAs using the aforementioned words, evidence, development and growth, but I should like to offer *mastery* as well.

The degree to which a child shows mastery of the CTAs may work for us. This is close to attainment or ability but has a certain optimism about it, a suggestion that we are all working towards mastering these character traits and attitudes.

Perhaps the most unhelpful phrase we hear in life generally, when talking about character development, is 'soft skills'. When people use this phrase I understand them to mean a person's personal attributes that enable them to build positive relationships with others – their social skills. Hard skills, by contrast, are usually taken to mean the visible, tangible skills needed to get the job done – procedural, technical, mechanical and so on. In a classroom context the hard skills might refer to the specific skills of literacy and numeracy, for example. You can see these in action and you can mark their efficacy right there on the page. Soft skills cannot be so easily measured. The word soft is so unhelpful here as it suggests softness or weakness as opposed to the strength inherent in those hard skills. This is ironic, isn't it, because for many people the idea of walking into a room of strangers and engaging with them, introducing oneself, communicating with them confidently and effectively and, perhaps, even motivating them, couldn't possibly be associated with weakness, quite the reverse. Huge amounts of courage are required for such things.

The phase 'character-building' suggests something more gritty – although, as I have indicated earlier in this book, such a phrase can be synonymous with some gruelling, soul-destroying exercise that can zap character rather than build it.

I attended a traditional grammar school up in North Yorkshire as a teenager. It's still there today. We were sent on 'character-building' cross-country runs every week, usually in the winter when the icy weather meant that the ground was too hard for rugby – the perfect conditions for a five mile run in a pair of cotton shorts and a t-shirt, of course.

The run consisted of three laps around a forest and back to school as quickly as you could, before the showers went cold or the bath was so cloudy it resembled broth.

I realised that if you hung back a little on the first lap, ducked into the forest itself and waited for a while, you could rejoin the rest of the runners as they completed the last half of the final lap. I did this every week very successfully, timing my return perfectly so that I was one of the stragglers at the back (the games masters had usually lost interest and gone inside by the time we weaklings rolled home, so it was fine). Being part of the last group meant the showers were freezing but even that was preferable to three complete laps of torturous running and crippling stitch, I judged.

On one occasion, I wasn't so lucky though. I mistimed my sneaky return, thought I was re-joining the stragglers at the back of the pack on the final lap, and then, as we neared the finish line, realised that I was just behind the leaders.

This was the day, as luck would have it, that the games master was running time trials and selecting runners for the county cross-country inter-school championships. He was the same games master who regularly enjoyed setting me 'character-building' challenges on rugby days too, which consisted mainly of being told to stand in the path of a kid three times my size, wait until he reached the speed of a juggernaut and then, like a suicidal frog on a motorway, hop in front of him, grab hold of a rhino-sized leg and pull him down on top of me. I still have the scars, both visible and invisible.

In assembly on the day after my poorly-timed cross-country run, I listened in horror as the headmaster proudly called out the names of the brave men and women who would be sent off to compete in the hills that encircled Giggleswick

School, where the championships were to be held that year. I'll never forget his expression as he rattled down the list only to pause incredulously at the name: 'Hammond?' One could hardly explain, 'No sir, you see, I was cheating, ha ha!'

I went to Giggleswick and came 147th out of about 150, I think. There were no convenient forests anywhere.

The character-building experiences of my traditional education were designed, I think, to give me grit and stamina in spade-loads, but I always felt they were somewhat mis-sold to me. On cricket days I was always known as Wally Hammond by the teachers, after the famous cricketer (whom none of the other kids had of and so they just assumed it was because Hammond was a wally).

Even now the phrase 'character-building' conjures up images of regimental games masters (mine was indeed ex-army) hurling 'words of encouragement' at you in lashing rain.

'It'll be good for you' is another well-known fib.

I am not averse to giving children challenges that will test their grit and resilience. Not at all. But I am against doing so in ways that seem to be devoid of positive encouragement and praise. 'This'll put hairs on your chest this will, but not if you cry.'

Perhaps there are alternatives to the phrase 'character-building' that don't sound so ominous. Challenging, invigorating, exciting, rewarding, action-packed, these all have a positive shine added. And the idea that anything that builds character must involve wearing almost no clothes and subjecting yourself to the winter winds or having some fifteen stone fifteen-year-old steamroller you, seems a little unimaginative.

But teachers know this today and they work hard to heap praise on any child who is able to scratch their way through a violin solo on a stage or represent the school in some spelling bee – or even sit still for an hour an a half in a silent examination room. And rightly so.

Character is not only tested in physical ways, it is about having the confidence to perform by yourself, to believe in yourself, to stand up and be counted or simply just to do the right thing when others around you are not.

So perhaps the following words will also help us to encourage, and comment on, children's performance character:

GRIT	gritty, tenacious, committed, courageous, plucky, resolute
ADAPTABILITY	adaptable, flexible, accommodating, open, tolerant
OPTIMISM	optimistic, resilient, positive, confident, enthusiastic, hopeful
SELF-CONTROL	composed, graceful, poised, reserved, in-control, self-directed, self-regulatory
EMPATHY	empathetic, understanding, considerate, compassionate, kind
DISCERNMENT	discerning, reasoned, rational, responsible, shrewd, astute, grounded, balanced
TRUST (Participativeness)	collaborative, cooperative, team-player, trusting, participative

Figure 5: Synonyms for use in formative observations and reports

I offer this list as a teacher who has so often searched for new synonyms when writing report after report after report at the end of term. As every teacher knows, if we are to observe and comment on the children's character development in an effective and bespoke way, and show evidence that we are adding value as teachers, then we need as wide a lexicon as possible. Such a vocabulary allows us to avoid any overuse of those words which do little for reporting on character traits and attitudes – words like performance, attainment and results – which focus primarily on the hard, visible skills we see demonstrated paper, like literacy and numeracy. The adjectives offered above describe 'invisible' attributes and attitudes – ones that are of great value both in school and beyond its gates. Soft skills, perhaps, but no less important.

5 Group dynamics

In his excellent chapter entitled 'Life in Classrooms' (*Teaching and Learning in the Primary School,* edited by Pollard and Bourne), Philip Jackson writes:

> Learning to live in a classroom involves, among other things, learning to live in a crowd... Most of the things that are done in school are done with others, or at least in the presence of others, and this fact has produced implications for determining the quality of a student's life.' (1994: 118)

I will discuss in much more detail the dynamics of the classroom in the sequels to this book – and especially in *Teaching for Communication* and *Teaching for Collaboration* – but it is worth exploring the nature of the classroom now, as it has significant impact on the development of a child's CTAs.

Remember Mary? Remember that courageous creativity she showed during wet playtime? And remember how the unintended side effects of the formal lesson that followed may have prevented such courageous creativity to continue to flourish, untrammelled?

I regularly deliver INSET or CPD training in school, and it is one of the most enjoyable and challenging aspects of my work. On occasion, I have set the teachers a task. Seated as they are in groups around tables, just like the children do, I provide everyone with a sheet of paper and a pencil. I then invite them (or tell them) to draw a picture of a horse.

Have you ever tried doing that? It is jolly difficult, I think. But have you ever tried

drawing a horse in front of your colleagues?

Even worse.

On other occasions, I have asked the teachers to write a short poem about the weather. Just a few lines, perhaps a haiku. As they write away, or stare blindly and very self-consciously at the paper, I sweep around the room, nodding approvingly and making encouraging noises to all and sundry.

That makes it even worse. Sharing your creativity like this in public requires some serious CTAs. It's a naked process that requires grit and spade-loads of self-confidence. It is not only about how much artistic talent you possess – if only it were that easy – it has much more to do with you the character traits and attitudes you have – the CTAs that will protect that artistic talent, ring-fence it and let it flourish in public: your optimism that the horse you are drawing will not look like a dog; your grit in persevering with the said 'dog' and not giving up on it, especially when the person next to you has already sketched a horse worthy of a Da Vinci sketch book; your trust that this is an activity worth participating in and one that won't make you look foolish...

And so on.

Learning rarely happens in solitary confinement and the social environment in which it takes place has huge impact on the results (or evidence!). As Labov says:

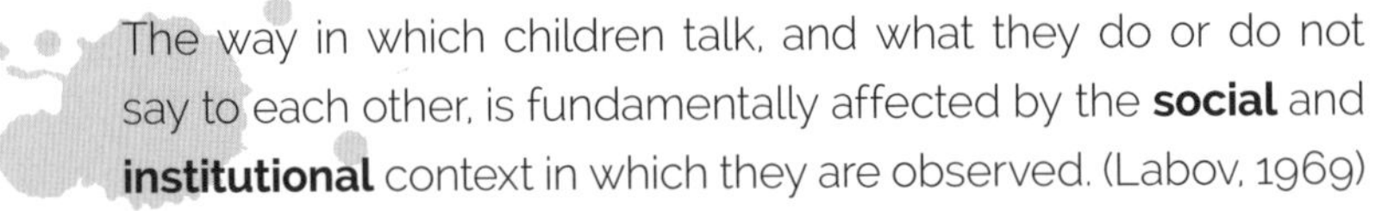

> The way in which children talk, and what they do or do not say to each other, is fundamentally affected by the **social** and **institutional** context in which they are observed. (Labov, 1969)

And the same is true of children's written communications and creative endeavours. The horse you draw, or the poem you write, will inevitably be affected by the creations of the person sitting next to you, but not only that, your work will be influenced by *your role* in the group. Are you the artist? Are you the poet? Or does some other lucky child in the class own that label and therefore can allow his or her talent to flow untrammelled. If you are not known to be an accomplished artist – perhaps you are the captain of the football team instead and famous for being 'sporty' and 'strong', then perhaps you may not consider it prudent to cause a stir by writing a beautiful poem or producing a sketch worthy of admiration. You might not want the hassle, or you might feel that it doesn't fit with your current profile.

Pigeon-holing goes on every day in every school and it's hard to run against the grain. In their superb book, *Group Dynamics in the Language Classroom*, Dornyei and Murphey (2003) paint a charming picture that may be recognisible to many teachers:

> In the early stages of a group's inception, pupils observe each other suspiciously, sizing up one another and trying to find a place in an unestablished and unstable hierarchy. They are on their guard, carefully monitoring their behaviour to avoid any embarrassing lapses of social poise. (Dornyei and Murphey, 2003: 14)

Did you think when you asked the children to begin writing their stories in class, or working through their maths equations, or drafting a history essay, or composing a piece of music, that the marks on the page would be an accurate measure of their talent or ability? Of course not. We all know that in addition to the task in hand, there are myriad other concerns at play, each of which will influence the end result on the page:

- is it my role in the group to be good at this?
- what if the teacher chooses to read my story out and it's either so good people tease me for being too keen, or it's so bad people laugh at me?
- will I get half way through this and then run out of ideas?
- how much longer 'til lunch?
- I wish Katie hadn't said what she said to me at breaktime
- Why's Ellie not talking to me, what have I done wrong now? She's *so* sensitive.
- I can't think of the right way to start this story
- I don't want Charlie to see this, in case it's rubbish
- Shall I start with some dialogue, that usually works
- I can't think of a good name for my lead character
- When's lunch?

And yet the words on the page will soon be marked and a grade may even be attached to them, giving an accurate measure of this child's story writing ability at the moment. This is reminiscent of classical science again, isn't it? What you see is what it is.

It would be impossible to take into account all of the social influences exerted on the child when marking her story. How on earth would that work?

And yet, we can consider the social context in which work takes place at the point when we plan for it and facilitate in class. We can consider the learning environment – and a key feature of this is the *group dynamics*. If we can get that right, we are removing yet another obstacle that is being placed in the way of this child's raw talent for writing stories.

We can consider our *class rules*.

Every school will have school rules and very often these are filtered down into classroom rules too. Some teachers will prefer a list of 'don'ts' where others will prefer a list of 'dos'; some will opt for a mixture. Some are called 'Golden Rules' –the idea being that if you break them you lose precious minutes from 'Golden Time', that liberating, if poorly timed, form period last thing on a Friday, when the decibels in the classroom soar and the teacher's patience plummets, bringing the week to a gloriously noisy end.

However the classroom rules are designed, and wherever they are displayed, I believe they must focus on the optimum growing conditions for children's character traits and attitudes to thrive. Precisely because we know that their character traits and attitudes – their CTAs – will always have huge impact on the quality and quantity of the visible work they produce, the stories they write, the pictures they draw and so on.

Mindful that every school will already have their own, may I offer a suggested set of rules.

Prior to working in education I worked in the legal profession, for a firm of solicitors up in Yorkshire, where I spent most of my days in the bowels of York Magistrates' Court, interviewing a list of delightful clients made up of mostly car thieves, burglars and jealous boyfriends with anger-management difficulties. Other days were spent in the York County Court, sitting in on acrimonious divorce proceedings, ancillary relief applications and child custody cases.

Such days imprinted the notion of balancing our own wants and needs with those of others indelibly on my mind, principally because everyday I met someone who was struggling with this balance. So my classroom rules, offered in Figure 1 below, are built around the scales – balancing the needs of the self against the needs of others. When rules are broken, one can easily see how the scales have tipped one way or the other, usually towards the self, though not always. Adhering to these rules may allow children's CTAs to flourish, which in turn will protect their natural talent, give it a boost, and allow it to flow, unhindered.

The Classroom Scales

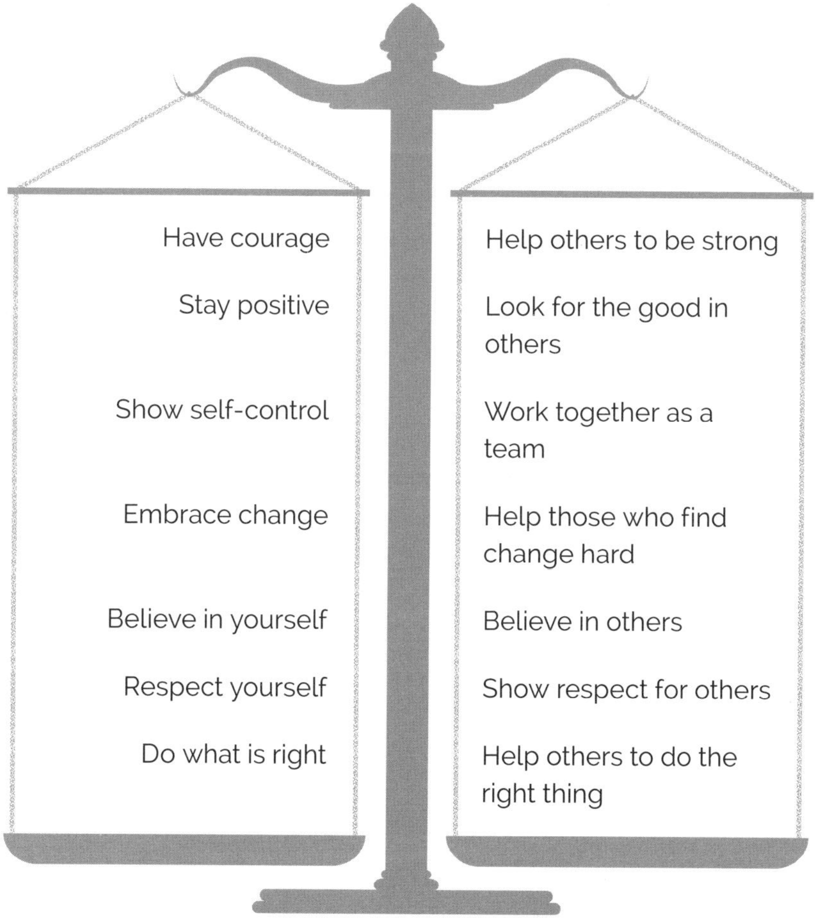

Have courage	Help others to be strong
Stay positive	Look for the good in others
Show self-control	Work together as a team
Embrace change	Help those who find change hard
Believe in yourself	Believe in others
Respect yourself	Show respect for others
Do what is right	Help others to do the right thing

Figure 6 – The Classroom Scales

I hope you can see how the children's CTAs feed into these rules.

It is interesting, isn't it, how all may schools regard such things as important, but fewer schools monitor the children's adherence to such rules in any organised and structured way. When they break a rule they will be picked up on it, quite rightly. But what happens when they apply the rules well? And is there a scale of getting better and better at these rules? Is there a progression? How do we know if a child is especially good at adapting to change or empathising with others?

Such rules for 'living in a crowd' could well be among the most important things a child will ever learn in their educational career; they are the behaviours and attitudes needed for them to prosper and find fulfilment at work and at home.

What is interesting too is how 'work' in school can sometimes contravene these rules, or remove the need for them.

Let's take the third one, for example: self-control. A great deal of how a school is structured is predicated upon managing the children's behaviour, and necessarily so, perhaps. As we discussed when considering young Mary earlier, the agenda, the seating arrangement, the timetable, the management of duties and the setting of tasks, these are all carefully planned for the Mary. So when is she put in a situation when she needs to show self-control? There is a difference between self-control and obedience, isn't there?

Let's take the fourth one too: embrace change. Again, I question when the children's ability to embrace change is ever tested? There will be some moments, of course, like the beginning of a new school year, the recruitment of a new teacher or the arrival of a new pupil, when the children's willingness to embrace change is challenged, but these are rare. The bulk of school life is meticulously planned to avoid uncertainty, as we considered in an earlier chapter.

The advantage of the scales is that they show, in a literal way, when behaviour within the group is tipped towards the self or towards others. It is worth purchasing a pair of traditional scales and displaying them in your classroom. They are a simple metaphor for how groups operate successfully, balancing the needs of individuals with the needs of the group.

As the DfE's *Teachers' Standards* state, teachers must:

> Have clear rules and routines for behaviour in classrooms, and take responsibility for promoting good and courteous behaviour both in classrooms and around the school, in accordance with the school's behaviour policy.

Have high expectations of behaviour, and establish a framework for discipline with a range of strategies, using praise, sanctions and rewards consistently and fairly.' (DfE, 2011: 12)

It seems to me to be a good idea to incorporate the scales into such a behaviour policy, and to use such a framework as evidence, again, that we are making efforts in the classroom to meet those standards.

Unlike the its visible cousin, the invisible curriculum cannot be taught and monitored without paying attention to the group dynamics of the classroom, since it is within such a group that the character traits and attitudes of the children are tested and developed. You can write a story or solve a maths equation in isolation, but you cannot develop your empathy in the same way; you need others around you. One can only develop trust in other people – enough to want to participate in something and not worry that your participation will end in Dornyei and Murphey's 'embarrassing lapses in social poise' – by being given the opportunities to collaborate. This cannot be done alone, like a maths examination can. You have to be in a situation with others. Fortunately the classroom is the ideal setting. Establishing those equitable classroom rules, based on balancing one's own needs with the needs of others, should help towards the development of trust, such an important CTA.

In the seventh title in this series, *Teaching for Interdependence*, I discuss in more detail the group *values* and *pledges* one might adopt in order to get the buy-in from students – creating an environment in which that trust allows them to collaborate effectively and confidently with one another.

Such group values are of great relevance to this book too, since they relate closely to the development of CTAs in children, and especially *trust*. So I offer them in summary here:

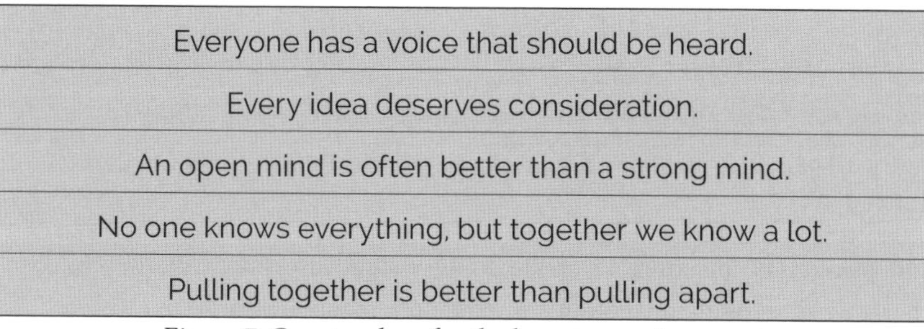

Everyone has a voice that should be heard.
Every idea deserves consideration.
An open mind is often better than a strong mind.
No one knows everything, but together we know a lot.
Pulling together is better than pulling apart.

Figure 7: Group values for the learning environment

These values are not rules exactly – we have the scales for that, based on the idea of a balanced justice within the group. Rather these values are important cornerstones for building the children's participativeness – seeing the value in joining in. They are core beliefs that will enable the children to work together and find synergy. These are related more to *performance character* rather than *moral character*, suggestions for building a positive attitude to learning collaboratively rather than a moral code to adhere to.

Having a positive attitude to the group and how it functions is of such importance, not only in school but in the workplace beyond education.

These values could be accompanied by *pledges* – each one showing how a value or core belief can and should be acted upon. For example:

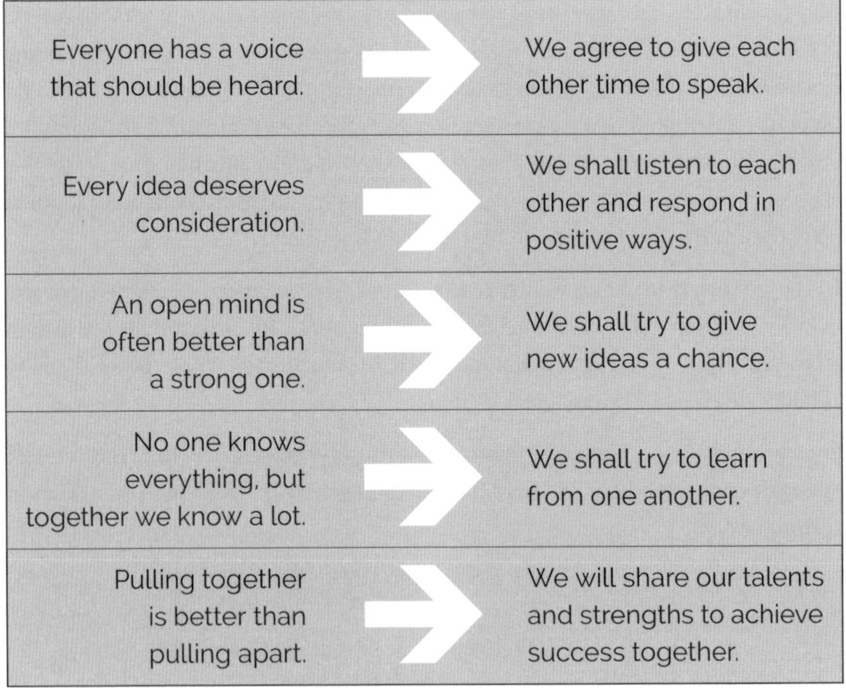

Figure 8: Group values with pledges for the learning environment

I shall resist suggesting that the children can be marked against these values and pledges in an effort to create some visible assessment of the children's character development, though some readers may wish to do so. Rather I see these as part of our efforts to establish the *learning conditions* most conducive to the development of character traits and attitudes, which is the central theme of this book. Such learning conditions must take into account the social dynamics of the classroom, of the school, because teaching and learning rarely happens in solitary confinement.

If learning how to live and work with others isn't an important goal for education that then I don't know what is.

6 Choices and challenges

Character development must be seen as an active rather than passive process, it must involve some decision-making on the part of the children if lessons learned are to last. They need to be felt and experienced. Fundamental to the notion of active learning is providing children with the opportunity to make *choices*. This is not to say I am advocating a liberal, *laissez faire* approach in which the child has total autonomy over their learning. There are many times when an authoritative rather than a dialogic approach is necessary! When a young child thumps his neighbour I am not a fan of sitting him down and saying, 'There are choices and consequence, Benjamin, and you have made a choice which will lead to some consequences that you won't like. So don't choose that option next time.'

Benjamin doesn't have an option here, there is no choice to be made. He is not allowed to thump his classmate.

But this is an extreme example and there are plenty of other scenarios we can create, inside the safety of the supervised classroom and within the safe parameters of the classroom rules, in which there are indeed choices to be made.

But if we want those character traits and attitudes to last longer than it takes to receive, remember and regurgitate some other constituent of the visible curriculum, then we have to involve the children in making decisions about how they will react and respond in a variety of safe situations.

The problem with so much of our formal education system is that it removes such decision making from the process altogether. Let's take the CTA grit as an example. I define grit as courage and tenacity in the face of adversity and the resolve to commit to long-term aims. There are myriad ways in which this can be tested in school if we stop to consider the moments when the children have a choice as to whether to show grit or not. But key to this section on choices and challenges is the idea that we are not simply presenting the children with a straight choice and highlighting the consequences for them: 'finish these maths questions and you'll get a good mark, give up and you won't.' Or 'finish that piece of writing and I'll be proud of you, leave it and I'll be cross'.

No teacher couches it in these terms, I am sure, but they may give this impression in the spoken and body language they make when work tasks are set. This is not what I am talking about. Any child always has the right to choose not to follow instructions or not to get on with any work. Giving children the opportunity to think independently and make autonomous choices does not mean do what I say or don't, it's up to you.

The choices and challenges I am referring to are those that are often bound up within *independent projects* – open-ended tasks in which you can truly see how much commitment a child shows, how much they believe in themselves, how much they care about their learning, and how much they can regulate they can manage their time and efforts.

Such projects will see the children exercising their own judgement in the choices they make and the working methods they adopt. As the DfE's *Teachers' Standards* state, a teacher must:

> Encourage pupils to take a responsible and conscientious attitude to their own work and study. (DfE, 2011: 10)

Independent projects like these, will help us to meet this standard and the work produced by the children can itself be used as evidence of the impact we as teachers have on our pupils' attitudes to learning and to their own efforts.

Work, or learning as I should say, comes in various forms in school but it can largely be summed up in two ways: activities that are carefully prescribed, with established learning goals, success criteria matched the to the curriculum and learning objectives, and designated time to complete them. Then there are those other activities that fall under the banner 'independent projects' – these may include researching, drafting, interviewing, collating evidence, composing, improvising, planning, making and collaborating with others. These are the tasks in which children feel a greater sense of ownership over what they are producing. Both types of assignment are important. Children need to learn to follow instructions to complete a piece of assessed work in class, just as they will need to follow orders at the adult workplace. But equally important is the need to be self-directed and self-motivated.

When I used to set a piece of work as an English teacher I was often aware that in the case of a reading comprehension exercise, for example, I chose the excerpt, I wrote the questions or chose them from a textbook, I planned which lesson the children would spend doing this and I was the one marking the work when it was finished. So in what way was this their piece of work? You could say it was mine. There was no choice about it, the work had to be done and if it wasn't then poor grades would ensue, not to mention a warning from me that they weren't working hard enough or making any effort. Such working practice is important but it's hard to see how it is *teaching*, rather than *training*. I think it is the latter. Train children how to do something, set them a task and then mark their efforts afterwards. This is training and responding, and it's important, but I don't believe it is teaching and learning. The opportunities for developing character traits and attitudes in children within training and responding sessions are somewhat limited, when compared with those that lie within teaching and learning.

Learning is something that children have to do for themselves, as every good teacher knows. It means more than responding to training, important though this is. It involves some decision making and independent action on the part of the child.

No matter what artistry we employ as teachers, learning is still something that learners have to do for themselves. (*Assessment for Learning*, Northern Ireland Curriculum)

We can only see those character traits and attitudes properly at play in learning when we set open-ended tasks, and ask open-ended questions. Research projects, creative writing tasks, mini-plays and re-enactments, these kinds of tasks will involve the children showing some grit to get the job done, even when they hit obstacles, or some discernment in the way they select their materials or choose their evidence. We are, in effect, setting tasks within which there are myriad choices to be made, and challenges to be faced. Here the choice is not simply, 'Shall I do what I'm told or not?' and the challenge is not, 'Can I do this difficult piece of work?' Rather the choices to be made relate to them personally, and the way they work. For example, let's take a research project in which the children need to produce a mini-project on the Amazon rainforest. The *choices* to be made might involve questions like:

- when shall I work on this project?
- how shall I set it out?
- how much text and pictures shall I use?
- shall I present this as a PowerPoint presentation instead?
- where shall I gather my research from?
- what particular aspects of the Amazon Rainforest shall I focus on?
- what key questions shall I use to structure my research?

And so on. The *challenges* faced in such a project will be numerous too, and may include, for example:

- negotiating some time on the family computer;
- getting the blessed printer to work;
- having the self-discipline and self-control to work instead of play;
- managing deadlines;
- recruiting the help of others if it is a group activity (and all that this entails in terms of cooperating with others);
- presenting one's project to the teacher and the class;
- sticking with it, even when it seems one is making little progress;
- having enough optimism to believe that the project will be any good anyway.

The finished assignment or presentation will be interesting in itself, but it will tell us a great deal more about a child's working practices and their character traits and attitudes to learning than a we might otherwise glean from a set piece of work in class, in response to some training given earlier in the lesson. We could see if they've been listening or not, I suppose.

As with most things in this book, it is not a question of *either/or*, it is *and*. We need to train the children in how to do something, or build their knowledge up, of course, and then we need to design how we shall measure their responses in class via some work set. But we also need to facilitate some independent thinking and learning which is best done by setting open-ended tasks and floating some questions that will challenge them cognitively and creatively. This is what I mean by choices.

7 The element of doubt

For some, this may be the most intriguing of the six elements of the learning environment offered in this book, since it may appear counter-intuitive to what education has always been about, which is about knowing rather than not knowing. It counters those historical assumptions about the purpose of education and indeed challenges the roles of teacher as the deliverer of established knowledge and student as the party charged with receiving, remembering and regurgitating it.

To be clear, in using the phrase 'element of doubt' I am not referring to the doubt that may exist in children's minds about their own ability – far from it. Neither am I referring to the doubt that may exist in teachers' minds about their own teaching capability. This is *self-doubt*, and it is not what I am referring to at all here, though of course it exists. What I am advocating is the idea of presenting the curriculum to pupils in a way which leaves open the possibility of questioning, scrutinising, challenging and thinking through the knowledge, skills and concepts that are so indelibly written into the visible curriculum. The doubt lies not in the pupils' ability to comprehend this knowledge, but in the knowledge itself.

It is possible to introduce such things at the same time as welcoming the children's own views on it and interpretations of it. What do *you* think? Would you agree? Is there a different way of doing this, or saying that? How do we *really* know this? Could a different conclusion be reached here? These are the questions which prompt not only learning but *understanding*.

I was fortunate enough to see a philosopher I have always admired, A. C. Grayling, speak at a Times Festival of Education at Wellington College a couple of years back. Of the many wise words he imparted and I hurriedly scribbled down, I distinctly remember him saying, 'Knowledge isn't only about facts, it's about opinion, interpretation, history, process of exploration. Education is not about the acquisition of knowledge, it's about the acquisition of understanding.'

As Grayling went on to say, one of the few obsolescence-proof things we can give children today is the ability to be a clear, deep thinker. Presenting knowledge in such a way that it remains open to scrutiny and deep thought seems to me to be a good idea in school. Doubt is a helpful tool in this regard, because it invites the children to think about what they are encountering rather than just slavishly accept it by rote. More meaningful learning comes from Grayling's process of interpretation and exploration.

Doubt is an emotive word with very obvious negative connotations. It might be associated with cynicism or skepticism, a defeatist attitude or a lack of self-belief. The phrase, Doubting Thomas (a reference to the apostle Thomas who refused to believe in the resurrection of Jesus until he had seen and felt the wounds inflicted upon Jesus from the cross for himself) has become an idiom for refusing to believe in anything unless you are shown proof. And this can be seen as a bad thing – showing a lack of imagination or faith. But is it, really? From a learning point of view, a certain unwillingness to accept knowledge or theories slavishly without satisfying the burden of proof for oneself is a jolly good thing, no matter how inconvenient it may be in the classroom. The most engaged pupils ask 'Why?' constantly.

The doubt I am referring to is that which gives rise to 'possibility-thinking', not defeatism, being curious rather than plain skeptical. I am talking about being open to the possibility that what we think we know is definite and indubitable, may not be. There may be other ways of doing things, other conclusions to be drawn, more knowledge to be learned that ultimately refutes a previously established view.

There are great figures in history we can draw on, who showed such doubt and an unwillingness to accept conventional views.

Leonardo Da Vinci had a difficult education, by all accounts. He famously described himself as an 'omo sanza lettere', an unlettered man. He was not undervaluing himself here, but rather was suggesting that in being unlettered he was uncluttered by the established views of others. As Charles Nicholls writes in his biography of Da Vinci, *The Flights of the* Mind, 'He believed he achieved his knowledge and understanding by observation and experience rather than by receiving it from others as a pre-existent opinion.' (Nicholls, 2004 : 55)

Nicholls goes on to quote Da Vinci himself: Those who merely 'quote' – in the sense of follow or imitate as well as cite – are 'gente gonfiata': they are, literally, puffed or pumped up by second-hand information; they are the 'trumpeters and reciters of the works of others'.

In citing this cry for experiential learning over the passive receipt of established wisdom of others, I am not advocating that formal instruction has no place in the learning classroom! But to introduce an element of doubt in what we say and how we say it is to extend an invitation to children to scrutinise knowledge introduced to them, to see it in context and to use their own experiences and observations to consider new possibilities. As Einstein famously said, 'We cannot solve our problems with the same thinking we used when we created them.' And yet it seems that the same conventional thinking is exactly what is being peddled in schools. It is only when an element of doubt is introduced into the learning classroom that we can encourage new thinking, debate and discussion, otherwise learning is nothing more than listening and mimicry – of the kind Da Vinci reeled against.

From the point of view of developing character traits and attitudes, doubt is a useful tool indeed. Certainty helps us little in developing grit, or adaptability or discernment. Such CTAs need situations in which they can be tested, not a classroom in which they lie dormant because every drop of uncertainty or doubt has been removed at the planning stage.

If we look at the great scientists in history, and today, it is their constant desire for the burden of proof that drives them on and tests their character. It is a need to reduce doubt that strengthens their resolve and commitment. We cannot wish for such character traits in the children if there was never any doubt to begin with.

It is at times when there has been no doubt at all that human progress has halted, and the pioneering spirit has dried up. Doubt is a catalyst for character development, when you think about it, and an absence of doubt can be the death of ambition. The great scientists in the past would not have made the discoveries they made if they had listened to their peers who said it couldn't be done, or there was nothing else left to know.

So what does this actually mean for teaching and learning? What of the wisdom (What I shall do on Monday)? We don't need to overhaul our entire curriculum and search only for facts that are in doubt! There is a canon of knowledge that we expect from a good education and which is wrapped up in a taught curriculum, and this should not change. But it is in the presentation of this knowledge where the real value lies. Mindful of the seven character traits and attitudes I have offered in this book, there are ways in which we can introduce an element of doubt into the learning environment and so give rise to a range of learning activities that will undoubtedly help us with character development.

Learning from giants

Consider how great names in each field, from science to music to sport, have handled *doubt*. How have they worked towards the elimination of doubt? What lessons can we learn from the working practices of past experts and high achievers? When we teach the great discoveries and achievements by Edison, Brunel, Darwin and so on, we should also consider how they worked, how they refused to accept that it couldn't be done, how their 'possibility-thinking' drove them on. Look for the milestones and pitfalls in the lives of great achievers, and the growth of their character traits and attitudes at that time. These are of equal importance to their discoveries.

Independent research projects

Set the children a range of independent projects that research the validity of theories made or conclusions drawn in the past. Use questions rather than factual statements: Was Thomas Edison the first person to think of a light bulb? Did everyone agree with Winston Churchill's judgement? Did Shakespeare write *all* his plays? Were the dinosaurs *really* wiped out by the effects of a giant asteroid strike?

Mock crime scene investigations

One often hears of the imaginative, courageous teacher who sketches the outline of a body on the floor of the playground and uses it to launch an investigation.

Police tape is used, with cones and all manner of authentic props to build excitement and belief. I think this is a little brutal myself, but I like the idea of introducing a 'who-dunnit' element into the learning environment and using it to ignite the children's curiosity. Historical crimes that have gone unsolved, or discoveries whose origins are the subject of controversy are ideal subjects for launching mock investigations at school. One might fake some new evidence that calls into question the authenticity of discoveries made, or pictures painted or works of fiction written.

Mock courtroom trials

Creating fictional scenarios in which the claims of great achievers - inventors, writers or explorers, for example – are questioned is an exciting way of introducing doubt and encouraging the children to search for the truth. After some research, a mock trial could be held, and great figures can be questioned on the validity of their claims. In most cases, of course, the achievements will be held to be true and just, but the process of investigating them will help children to develop that all-important discernment and empathy and trust.

'What if?' essays

In addition to teaching the great discoveries made, landmarks conquered or political decisions made, it is worth asking the children to consider the consequences of such moments *not* happening. What if the light bulb had not been invented? What if evolution had not been so brilliantly articulated by Darwin? What if the second world war had not happened? What if Einstein had never lived?

Contingency plans

Everything is so meticulously planned in school, and it has to be that way. We are brain surgeons, after all. Our operations take terms rather than hours, but the responsibility is the same and this means careful planning.

But children would benefit from the chance to join in some contingency planning for fictional scenarios, in which something we depend upon fails or disappears. What if the heating failed or the water supply ran out in school? What if the cookers in the kitchen broke? What if there were a power-cut that lasted a month? What if the rules we established to run our school turned out to be the wrong ones? All these questions, and many more, can help us to develop character traits and attitudes in the children, as they learn to adapt, predict, hypothesise and work together to solve problems and plan for futures that are not as predictable, not as certain, as we thought.

The element of doubt allows us, as teachers, to emphasise the important point that none of us know everything there is to know, and even what we do know may be subject to debate. When the future seems predictable and dependable, that is usually the moment when we are surprised by something out of the blue.

A search for more knowledge depends on the idea that we don't know everything and there are new things to know, new ways of working, playing and living, new theories to be discovered that refute older ones. This is the joy of learning. Casting doubt and scrutinising evidence, this is a fundamental part of learning and, if managed carefully, it can deepen understanding and raise engagement in the classroom.

8 Observation

Fundamental to any essay on observing the invisible curriculum at work in schools is the idea that children, like all humans, react to the environment in which they find themselves. That sounds rather obvious doesn't it – of course we react to our environment. But when you think about it, how much opportunity is there in school to monitor the way children react to their surroundings? How much attention is paid to creating the right environment, the right conditions, that will produce the most positive and productive reaction from the children? There are other factors that can often take precedence: budget, health and safety, security, time efficiency, class size, timetabling issues, and so on. It would be hard to envision a school in which these factors are not so important, of course they are.

And yet I am certain that the physical and social environment outside children's heads has a significant impact on what goes on inside them. I am no more a psychologist than I am a quantum physicist, but I have taught for many years and I have seen children react in certain ways in response to the physical space and the social context in which they are taught. It may be easier for all of us if children reacted to what we are telling them in identical ways, regardless of where we are telling them it, and who else is listening in, but they don't.

Put a child in a large examination room and there is a likelihood that they will react differently to if they were in a small classroom. Just as some teachers perform quite differently when giving an assembly to the whole school, compared with their performance in their own classroom – this is more common than you might think.

Ask a child a question alone and his response will be markedly different to that which is given when exactly the same question is posed to him in front of his peers, or other teachers, or in assembly before the whole school. Chat to him casually on a bench at playtime and both his body language and his speech will differ from what you see and hear when he is standing by your desk at the front of the classroom.

This is obvious, isn't it?

Ask a child to write a story at home, and it may be quite different to the story he writes in class, and significantly different from the story he writes whilst being timed and sitting at desk number fifty-three in the centre of a large sports hall crammed with other desks and other candidates.

If the same question, or task, prompts very different responses depending on the physical and social environment in which it is set then clearly something invisible is happening here. Again, this will be apparent to any teacher.

But if the fact that the quality and quantity of a child's response to a task set differs depending on where, when and with whom he is working, then how is this recognised in the way we monitor, assess and report on that child's progress through school? Where does it feature in our observations?

I can't imagine attending a parents evening and hearing the teacher say, 'Yes, I know your son only achieved a C grade in Geography this term, but you should see the state of the classroom!' Or, 'Yes, he scored a C in the exam, but you should have heard the whispering going on behind him, it was so distracting, or the wind outside, or the fact that the heating wasn't functioning properly and his little hands were shaking while he wrote.'

It's always more black and white than that, isn't it? He is a boy. He is aged twelve. This is an exam designed for twelve year olds. This is the expected level and this is what he got. Sorted. (Okay, and is there a specific time of year when these sheep should be shorn too? Let me know and I'll take him to the barbers for a twelve-year-old's haircut).

To place every piece of work, or every examination result, in its wider context would be impossible. We would need not only to recognise that a pupil has managed a C in Geography: he has also managed to adapt to the physical and social environment of the geography classroom; he has managed to adapt his responses to fit into the standards expected by his Geography teacher, which may be different to those of other teachers; he has learned to sit still and concentrate long enough to put something down on paper; he has learned to ignore the distractions of others; he has learned to battle on, even if he can't understand it; he has learned to switch very quickly, within minutes, from a Maths lesson in which he was simplifying fractions to a Geography lesson in which he was labelling a diagram of a glacial valley.

He has, in summary, developed his *performance character* at the same time as showing us what he *knows* in Geography. But such growth is eclipsed by the standard termly attainment grade that shows us only what he knows (or has remembered).

Some schools do offer termly grades for effort too, in each subject, but it is difficult to know exactly upon what criteria such grades are based. Is a grade 1 for effort (the highest score) awarded for maximum effort or best behaviour? If it is for maximum effort, how does anyone know what that child's maximum effort looks like? And if we don't know that, how can we say he has earned a top grade?

Of course, we know that his position on the leaderboard for this subject (his rank position in the class or set) is often taken to describe his performance too. Some might be think it *is* his performance. But it's not, as I have suggested earlier.

It would be unwieldy to say the least if, for every subject in the school curriculum, we sent to parents at the end of term an attainment grade, an effort grade, and a grade for every one of the following: grit, self-control, adaptability, discernment, and so on. But the invisible curriculum is as important as the visible one; the way we adapt to our environment, the way we cope with change, the way we handle difficult situations and the way we value ourselves and our own contributions *matters* very much.

I am arguing for two things here: firstly that the invisible curriculum, and specifically children's character traits and attitudes to learning, are borne in mind when we assemble the physical and social surroundings of our schools – the growing conditions; and secondly, that we find a way of *observing* and *reporting* on those CTAs as the child moves up through the school – we consider the observable aspects of the child's performance character and we report on them, not with a grade necessarily, but in a little more detail than perhaps we do at the moment.

There is currently no real mechanism for observing and reporting on the children's character development at the same time as their academic development

– despite them being inextricably linked. There is currently no mechanism for monitoring their interactions in the class other than to say they 'worked well' or remained 'on task' or 'behaved themselves'. Obviously these things attract comments in the end of term report, and especially the tutor report, but they can often be rather generalized: 'Mary has worked well this term' or 'Tom sets a good example to his peers'. The language referenced in the previous chapter may assist here (although none of the words offered would have been new to the mindful, reflective teacher!).

In the Early Years Foundation Stage, there is so much good practice going on that we can learn from in this regard. One of the things I like most about EYFS is the repeated use of the word 'evidence' and the need to collect evidence of development from parents, from other relevant adults, from the child and from observational materials. The assessment criteria is delightfully child-centred, as you might expect, and I believe it has as much relevance to a nine-year-old, or fourteen-year-old, as it does to a five-year-old.

EYFS staff are required to observe the children:

- Finding out and exploring
- Using what they know in their play
- Being willing to have a go
- Being involved and concentrating
- Keeping on trying
- Enjoying achieving what they set out to do
- Having their own ideas
- Using what they already know to learn new things
- Choosing ways to do things and finding new ways.

Can you think of a better list of observables in children at school?

Is it workable to have a system of monitoring *performance* as well as *results* as the children rise through the school? Can the CTAs be tracked in this way, without grading them? Yes, I believe all these things are achievable, we just need to shift our thinking with regard to results and evidence. As the EYFS Handbook (2014) states:

> Observational assessment involves reaching an understanding of children's learning by watching, listening and interacting as they engage in everyday activities, events and experiences, and demonstrate their specific knowledge, skills and understanding. It is the most reliable way of building up an accurate picture of children's development and learning, especially where the attainment demonstrated is not dependent on overt adult support. Observational assessment is key to understanding what children really know and can do. Some observations will be planned but some may be a spontaneous capture of an important moment.

What a delightful phrase: 'a spontaneous capture of an important moment'. Perhaps this is what I was hoping for when viewing my children's exercise books on parents evening, and feeling that they had not captured much of the excitement that I knew was going on in the classroom.

But as much as I admire the spirit of this excerpt from the EYFS Handbook, I confess to feeling some disappointment over the inclusion of the sentence 'Observational assessment is key to understanding what children really know and can do.' Why stop there? Why are we only observing what the children *know* and can *do*? Is this really what defines us as we grow older? Perhaps it is, but it shouldn't be. Perhaps too many of us define ourselves and others by what we know and can do. What about *how* we are, *who* we are, how we collaborate with others, how we face challenges, how much we believe in ourselves, how positive we feel? These attitudes and aptitudes may have little to do with our knowledge and skills and yet it is the latter which receives so much of our attention. Perhaps there is a missed opportunity here: I embrace the notion of observation in this excerpt, but I feel that, yet again, we are observing only a fraction of the child and their development if restrict ourselves to looking for knowledge and skills only.

But the idea of spontaneously capturing those important moments is very much what I mean by the word *evidence* rather than *results*. Replacing the word assessment with observation, helps us to shift from testing to watching, from summative to formative, if you like.

In many schools today not only are IEPs (Individual Education Plans) offered to children in receipt of learning support or acceleration/extension, ILPs (Individual Learning Plans) may be offered to every child. Often, though not always, such IEPs or ILPs may set targets that are not only focused on knowledge and skills to be learned, but also on character traits and attitudes to learning – pupils' habits of mind.

An ILP for every child may be too much for some schools, especially those with very large classes, but many schools will have ways of tracking the behaviours, character traits and attitudes of the children in addition to their academic progress. Some suggestions for doing this might include:

- alphabetised ring-binders, with one page for each child, in which formative comments can be recorded by the teacher(s) under certain headings pertaining to the invisible curriculum, and the CTAs specifically;
- a system of stickers or badges, rewarding the character traits, attitudes or behaviours that lead to *active* learning. Readers will have their own ideas on designs and style, but the content might include:

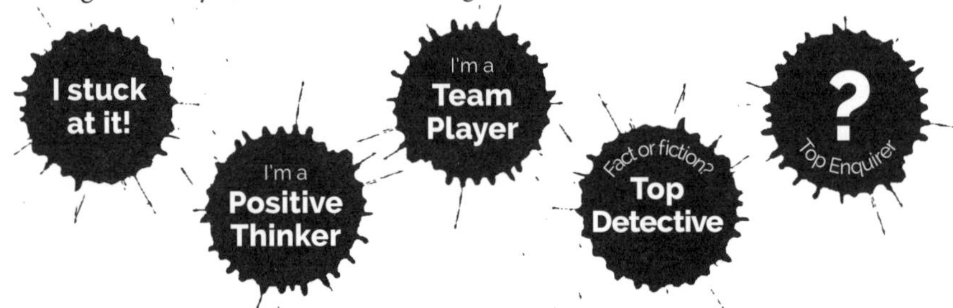

- a learning profile, again divided into headings reflecting the character traits and attitudes recognised as valuable in learning, held on the school's intranet, in which formative comments can be uploaded against pupils' names, perhaps at the end of a lesson or end of a day;
- page-spreads in pupils' diaries or planners – in which teachers can record comments, award stars or place ticks to show the development or growth of CTAs in children (notice I have resisted using the word 'progress' here, since this indicates movement towards an established standard!).

All these suggested methods of recording observations of the children's 'invisible ink' assume one knows what to look for in terms of character traits and attitudes as they develop, and we yet know that, as with any aspect of the invisible curriculum, this may not always be so apparent. In Figure 8 below I offer some examples of behaviours shown or comments made that may indicate positive growth in character traits and attitudes, and therefore warrant some recognition from the teacher:

CTA	Evidence of growth
Grit	Completing a difficult project or extended piece of work; Finishing a race or physical challenge; Continuing to learn a musical instrument and passing a grade; Solving a particularly difficult maths question; Finally mastering a tricky times-table; Completing a piece of artwork; Surviving an adventure camp; Achieving personal targets on IEP/ILP; Coping well with an injury.
Adaptability	Coping well with a new timetable at the end of a first week; Handing all homework in on time; Settling well into a new class or school; Coping well with a change of teacher or personal tutor.
Optimism	Taking criticism well; Bouncing back from bad news; Auditioning for a part in a play; Entering competitions; Responding well to advice given; Showing self-belief when facing challenges; Showing enthusiasm for learning and bettering oneself.

Self-control	Showing restraint when others are hurtful; Showing good organizational skills and self-direction; Never complaining when facing difficult situations; Resisting the temptation to join in unacceptable behaviour.
Empathy	Helping others in difficulty; Welcoming a new pupil and being a good buddy; Responding well in PSHE / citizenship lessons; Working well in paired or group work; Showing consideration for others.
Discernment	Doing the right thing; Understanding the difference between fact and opinion; Writing a good discursive essay; Performing well in debates and discussions; Showing good judgement in times of difficulty or challenges.
Trust (participativeness)	Joining in group activities; Working well with others; Participating in competitions and challenges; Being a good team player in sports; Performing in group plays and school productions; Contributing in class discussions.

Figure 9: Observable evidence of character development in pupils

Conclusion

Writing in the Guardian in 2011, Sir Anthony Seldon, Master of Wellington College, wrote:

> Through no fault of the teachers – the relentless pressure of league tables has dictated schools sacrifice so much of the education of the whole child for the sake of exam grades. … Development of character in young people is not at the cost of academic performance: instead, evidence shows it boosts exam results.

I have repeated the mantra throughout this book, it's not 'either/or', it is 'and'. That is to say, when we pay attention to the development of children's character traits and attitudes, we facilitate *dual learning* – developing character traits and attitudes at the same time as developing academic intelligence. We raise standards in the visible curriculum by paying attention to the invisible learning going on. For example, the benefits to academic performance of developing grit or discernment or self-control are obvious.

Such dual learning, where children are learning performance character traits as well as academic knowledge, has always happened, of course. In every classroom, in every school, children are not only learning from the visible curriculum, they are learning from the invisible one too. But perhaps a great deal of the latter is done subconsciously, as an adjunct to the 'real' work that goes on and which yields those visible grades. One cannot divorce one from the other, it is precisely in the blending of both when children learn most effectively.

But there are benefits for the teacher too, when we pay attention to the invisible curriculum because it is precisely those moments when we see children's grit or optimism or empathy growing that we may find the most satisfaction as educators. We are privileged to be there, present, when children's character development takes another important leap forward: when they show some courage and complete an arduous task or challenge, when they help a fellow pupil in difficulty, showing empathy and understanding, when they show some optimism and belief in their own ability, or when a team pulls together and achieves success. These moments remind us why we went into the profession in the first place. Such edifying moments happen frequently in schools but often they are eclipsed by the constant need to show visible signs of academic progress. This takes up so much of our thoughts and concerns, but it would be impossible to facilitate academic progress without building character too.

Whenever a teacher is teaching from the visible curriculum, she is always teaching invisible lessons too, whether she knows it, or likes it, or not. It would be absurd to suggest that a mathematical concept or some language technique can be taught to children without, at the same time, conveying messages to them about their attitudes to learning. We are, after all, human beings and although great emphasis is being placed on children's computational capacity at the moment – VR and NVR scores are so fashionable aren't they? – such capacity cannot possibly sum up a child's true potential. Verbal reasoning requires a child to shut off a great many of their innate capacities and faculties and concentrate most keenly on the task in hand. Any distraction, any day-dreaming, can render a child's IQ to be measurably lower than that of the child who can focus more keenly and hold a phrase or sum or pattern in his head. Clearly this is an important skill to master. Try holding down a successful job, in just about any field, if you cannot concentrate for periods of time.

But concentration isn't intelligence, is it?

The language we use to describe intelligence often seems to suggest speed and efficiency, doesn't it: quick, sharp, switched on, alert, decisive, clued up, and so on. But there are so many moments in our lives when such rapid processing has little or no value at all, in fact it can positively cause us trouble. Major decisions in our lives often require something else other than quick-thinking; they require reflection, consideration, an understanding of others, self-control, discernment.

Though it may be convenient to measure children's verbal reasoning or mathematical abilities and then rank them in order of 'intelligence', clearly this is only a fraction of what is actually going on in the learning environment, or occurring within the developing child.

The scale and pace of technological advancement and the sheer speed with which we communicate and live our lives as a result, may suggest that the ability to process and retain information very quickly is a valuable skill in the workplace beyond school. I know this to be true. But why are we racing computers in this way? Why are we trying to increase the speed with which a child can apply logic? What is that for? I have the stilted emails from colleagues to prove that speed is, apparently, everything and we all need to make decisions *now.* Online communication is all about gleaning meaning from the page as quickly as possible and responding as speedily as you can; there is no place for empathy or emotional intelligence, and I know a lot of serial emailers who are quite happy about that, given the brevity and frequency of their missives. They have a thought and email it; they seem to be shutting down all possibility of reflection.

Many of the ways in which we currently assess children's learning ability do seem to suggest that fast and efficient processing of text and data is everything. But it's not. The dominance of such types of intelligence test may be leading us to a very narrow, skewed view of what it means to be intelligent. Are we sleep-walking into a time when success in school is measured in computational capacity and processing speed? Have we already reached it? This may have disastrous consequences for everyone, ultimately.

I don't believe Homo sapiens have lasted so long on this Earth because of our ability to process numbers quickly or hold a rational thought without being distracted. Rationality may even be a recent phenomenon. Reasoning is something of a Western obsession, after all. We have survived as a species precisely because we possess the very skills and faculties that have no place in a verbal reasoning exam and cannot be reduced to a formulae or code, or even expressed in words and numbers: being sensitive, reactionary, open to opportunity, empathetic, instinctive, intuitive, imaginative, creative, collaborative and so on. Shut those things off and you render yourself entirely exposed to danger – and devoid of any ability to make an independent decision, not to mention sustain a meaningful relationship. We need a mixture of intelligences, don't we? If we only test our abilities using words and numbers, or worse, attempt to *summarise* our ability in words and numbers, we risk missing so much of what it means to be human. We need to recognise the value of our senses, our emotions, our motivation and our *character*.

How does a 125 in verbal reasoning reveal a child's fortitude? How does a 135 in non-verbal reasoning reveal a child's optimism? Unless that child is hoping to be a computer when he grows up, I suggest he will need these traits, and many more that aren't subject to logic or reason. A cynic might go further and suggest that verbal and non-verbal reasoning tests only tell us who is and isn't educable: who possesses the ability to sit still and concentrate on something without being distracted, who can follow logical instructions to the letter or apply a formula and do what they're told to achieve an expected outcome. No wonder such tests have become so fashionable in education today, and especially for school-entry pre-tests.

Education should be an aesthetic experience but tests like these help to make it an anesthetic one. 'Shut off as many of your natural inclinations and capacities as you can and you'll concentrate better on this verbal analogy or this algebraic equation, or you'll crack this code more efficiently.'

I have a computer for applying logic, and it does it in a fraction of the speed. But I don't think my computer can empathise with my friend when she feels aggrieved or comfort my son when he feels scared.

Only the invisible curriculum can teach you how to do that.

References

Baggot, J. (2011) *The Quantum Story.* Oxford: University Press

Blatchford, R. (2014) *The Restless School.* Woodbridge: John Catt Educational Limited

Bruner, J. (1977) *The Process of Education.* US: Harvard University Press

Christodoulou, D. (2013) *Seven Myths About Education.* London: Routledge

Covey, S. R. (1989) *The 7 Habits of Highly Effective People.* London: Simon & Schuster.

Dewey, J. (1915) *The School and Society & The Child and the Curriculum.* BN Publishing

Dornyei, Z. and Murphey, T. (2003) *Group Dynamics in the Language Classroom.* Cambridge: University Press

Gelb, M. (1998) *How to think like Leonardo Da Vinci.* New York: Bantam Dell

Locke, J. (1693) *Some Thoughts Concerning Education and Of the Conduct of the Understanding* Indiana: Hackett Publishing Company

Montessori, M. (1949) *The Absorbent Mind.* Adyar: The Theosophical Publishing House

Nicholls, C. (2004) *Leonardo Da Vinci – The Flights of the Mind.* London: Penguin

Piaget, J. (1969) *The Psychology of the Child.* New York: Basic Books.

Pollard, A. and Bourne, J. (ed) (1994) *Teaching and Learning in the Primary School.* London: Routledge.

Robinson, K. (2001) *Out of Our Minds.* Chichester: Capstone Publishing Limited

Rousseau, J. (1762) *Emile or On Education.* New York: Basic Books Inc. (1979)

Seligman, M. E. P. (2006) *Learned Optimism – How to Change you Mind and Your Life.* USA: Vintage Books

Spender, S. (1985) *Collected Poems 1928 – 1985.* London: Faber and Faber Limited

Tough, P. (2014) *How Children Succeed.* London: Arrow Books

Forthcoming titles in the Invisible INK series

Teaching for Creativity

Teaching for Motivation

Teaching for Curiosity

Teaching for Thinking Skills

Teaching for Communication

Teaching for Interdependence